UNSTOPPABLE

UNSTOPPABLE

Finding Hidden Assets
to Renew the Core
and Fuel Profitable Growth

———

CHRIS ZOOK

Harvard Business School Press
Boston, Massachusetts

Library of Congress Cataloging-in-Publication Data
Zook, Chris, 1951-
  Unstoppable : finding hidden assets to renew the core and
fuel profitable growth / Chris Zook.
      p. cm.
  Includes bibliographical references.
  ISBN-13: 978-1-4221-0366-1 (hardcover : alk. paper)
  ISBN-10: 1-4221-0366-8
  1. Corporations—Growth. 2. Strategic planning. 3. Organizational
change. 4. Corporate profits. 5. Industrial management. I. Title.
  HD2746.Z664 2007
  658.4'012—dc22

                                                    2006038270

The paper used in this publication meets the minimum requirements of the
American National Standard for Information Sciences—Permanence of Paper
for Printed Library Materials, ANSI Z39.48-1992.

Contents

Acknowledgments

My first thanks must go to the clients of Bain & Company, who allow my partners and me to participate in an extraordinary range of businesses in every stage of the focus-expand-redefine cycle and in every corner of the globe. As this book documents, the speed of business is increasing and the job of a senior executive in a major company becomes more complex and stressful every day. I am deeply appreciative for the support and help of our clients in a myriad of ways.

I also thank all my partners at Bain & Company. More than a hundred of them have contributed ideas, time, contacts, results from their own work, advice, guidance, articles, or access to their most precious asset: their clients. As a group they have been supportive at all times of my efforts on this book and the two that came before it. I especially thank my new colleagues in Bain's Amsterdam office, and office head Raj Pherwani, for their tolerance and support of a newly arrived partner trying to juggle work on the book with client work in the region.

It is difficult to know whom to acknowledge by name, because there is no truly logical cutoff point. However, some partners have gone far out of their way in their support, interest, willingness to read draft after draft, and sharing of key insights. The last three managing directors of Bain—Tom Tierney, John Donahoe, and

Steve Ellis—have given me the support throughout to complete this series of books even as it sometimes cut into other things I could have been doing in the firm. I thank them for their trust. Orit Gadiesh, Bain's chairman, has given her encouragement and advice throughout.

Steve Schaubert has been an inspiration, a mentor, and a tireless reader of all drafts of every book. Darrell Rigby always seemed to find the time in an impossible schedule to read drafts and send extensive thoughtful e-mails that invariably redirected my thinking. Jimmy Allen, co-head with me of Bain's Strategy Practice and co-author of *Profit from the Core,* was a constant source of ideas and energy. Keith Aspinall and Fred Reichheld also contributed significant thoughts and ideas along the way.

Research support and ideas flowed continuously from the Bain team that is charged with supporting the Strategy Practice. That team has been led ably by Rachel Corn, who has read every version of this book and has shaped or conducted many of the key analyses, especially the *Fortune* 500 tracking study. I also thank the long line of brilliant consultants who staffed the teams and generated hundreds of modules and case studies for Bain & Company that I drew on.

Marci Taylor has supported research on all three of the books and has done some of the key analyses, such as the one on the value of market leadership, that are referenced in every book. She has also read every draft of every book. Whew.

The Bain library staff, especially Bill Dwyer and Ralph D'Angelo, has been fast and creative in constantly helping me assemble accurate financial data or locate obscure historical facts in support of the work. I am deeply grateful to these competent professionals.

Wendy Miller, head of marketing at Bain, has assembled a great team that has helped me on messaging, writing, ideas, examples, and editing. I especially thank Katie Smith Milway, director of publishing, and Cheryl Krauss, director of public relations. In addition, John Case, an extended member of Katie's team, devoted considerable time to restructuring and rewriting parts of an early version of the book, leaving indelible prints on it. Kascha Piotrzkowski carefully doublechecked the accuracy of the book's facts with the support of Samantha Peck, who helped validate our many company stories and executive quotes. Susan Donovan was amazing as the "keeper of the master draft" and, at the end, choreographing countless edits from over a dozen places, as well as making many further improvements along the way.

Melinda Adams Merino, senior editor at Harvard Business School Press, has been my copilot for all three of the books I have written. Melinda marshaled a fantastic team of specialists from cover design to technical editing, including production editor Marcy Barnes-Henrie. Whenever I was stuck, her team always had the right insight on the direction to go; whenever I lost focus, they got me back on course. Their brilliance constantly rescued me from dead ends or dead prose. Thank you!

Brenda Davis has been my assistant through this entire three-book odyssey. She has seen every draft of every chapter, has prepared and polished the manuscript, has dealt with the complex logistics of scheduling to get all this done, and has counseled me psychologically through the process. In the last round she even moved to Amsterdam, where I now spend most of my time, to help me adjust to a new environment and to get the book done.

I have done about fifty interviews, mostly with CEOs, during the course of writing this book. I am deeply grateful to these busy executives, who took the time to host me at their companies, tell me their stories, and share their ideas. My greatest fear is that I have not captured fully the insights that reside in their comments and experiences.

Finally, there is my family, particularly Donna, my wife of more than thirty years. During the course of this book she moved with me to Amsterdam and fought her way through a temporarily disabling health condition. Her positive energy was unstoppable. Through it all, she remained a selfless supporter of this project, giving me space, time, and encouragement to "get it done," as she has through the course of my career and three book projects in seven years. My boys, Andrew and Alex, provided inspiration to write these books and gave me a stream of contemporary analogies to use in the book and in speeches. When I took things too seriously, my family kept me grounded in reality. Thank you.

Introduction

Something has changed fundamentally in the world of business. Although few people seem to have internalized this shift, the effect is startling and profound. Ten years from now, one in three companies will no longer be independent because of bankruptcy or takeover, and another one in three will be completely different at its core, maybe even having a different core. Only one in three will resemble what it looks like today.

What is this change? It seems that for a majority of businesses today, fundamental threats to the core have moved from rare events to nearly common occurrences. And most businesses are not prepared for what that means. In many industries, it appears that the weather patterns of business have changed from a temperate climate punctuated by periodic storms to a norm of frequent storms punctuated by periodic monsoons. Will this situation be true forever? Possibly, but who knows? What is certain is that it will be the case over the next decade.

My first two books with Harvard Business School Press—*Profit from the Core* (2001) and *Beyond the Core* (2004)—were about the search for sustained and profitable growth. This body of work over a five-year period studied how often companies fail to recognize the full potential of their core business and, as a result, prematurely abandon it in the pursuit of hot markets or sexy new ideas, only to realize their error—often, when it is too late. The books described a systematic way to assess your full potential and to make sure that you do not fall into this common, and typically human, trap.

Yet what happens when the core itself comes under severe threat? How do you recognize the magnitude of that threat before it is too late? How do you make sensible changes in the fundamentals of your business to reignite a new wave of growth rather than risk stalling or even worse? What do you do when it seems that your success formula is starting to reach a limit sooner than you expected?

How to make fundamental change in your business model, while still running your business, is what this book is about. It is about how all businesses ultimately approach a natural limit to their growth formulas, something that demands changes in strategy or even in the core itself. Why then is this book called *Unstoppable?* Shouldn't its title reflect endings, rather than persistence? The reason for the title is that the companies we chose to study and profile most closely are those that beat the odds. We also analyzed patterns of failure and estimated the odds of success offered by various paths in various situations. Many of those statistical findings are reported throughout the book. But in the narrative, we focused on the case studies and accounts of the executive teams that, for a period of years, fought their way through severe threats to their core and found a way to renew their trajectory of profitable growth.

This does not mean that these companies are forever unstoppable. No company is. In fact, our data suggests that an increasing percentage of companies will experience fundamental threats to their core strategies as the world speeds up. Strategies are becoming obsolete faster than ever before. But the companies we feature found a way to go from unsustainable to unstoppable, against the odds, for a significant period.

The central finding brings with it a positive and surprising message. Virtually all the success stories built their renewal on a company's "hidden assets," which previously had been undervalued, unrecognized, or underutilized. These hidden assets were not central to the strategy of the past, but they held the key to the future. Furthermore, the older and more complex the company, the greater was the likelihood of finding promising hidden assets. This does not mean that new capabilities, ideas, or technologies from outside your four walls are not critical ingredients—quite the contrary. But it does mean that many companies already hold most of the cards for a winning hand but do not realize it. It is a lot easier to win in poker—a game also blending skill, luck, and intuition—if you know that you already hold a few aces than if you are relying on the dealer for a whole new set of cards.

The alternatives to looking deep within your own core to redefine your strategy prove to be much more risky. They include entering the race for the next hot market, or buying in to the lottery for the next big technology, or bidding in the auction for the next big transforming acquisition, or hoping that your company miraculously will become more "innovative," thereby neutralizing the strategic threat without even confronting it. Although these routes sometimes lead to fame and fortune, we find that the odds of success are low and the risks to the organization are often high. To rely on these risky pathways alone is to fall under the spell of seductive, but dangerous, siren songs.

My conviction to write this book crystallized at the annual partner meeting for my firm, Bain & Company. At this meeting each industry practice group holds day-long sessions to describe its point of view on the dynamics of its industry and on the strategies being followed by various competitors. As I wandered from room to room, sampling presentations, something began to dawn on me. Almost all our clients and their competitors were confronting more fundamental and more frequent threats to their core businesses— requiring much broader thinking about the strategies of the future—than before. It was true in airlines, where low-cost carriers were finally triggering fundamental moves by the majors. It was true in media, where businesses from film production to newspapers were seeing their success formulas of past decades hitting the wall and seeing their stock prices tank. It was true in telecommunications, where convergence and the Internet were causing seismic shifts, and where once-impregnable fortresses such as AT&T had fallen and been acquired, and the foundations of the new fortresses were still shaky. It was true even in many basic industrial businesses, which were encountering new levels of turbulence, often related to the emergence of competitors in China and its ripple effect on supply chains and cost structures around the world.

I felt this acutely, as it relates to the topic of this book, when I was on a bus visiting Suzhou Industrial Park outside Shanghai. Suddenly, out the window I saw a long dark band, like a Möbius strip, winding its way around many buildings. What was it? As the bus moved closer, I realized that the dark band was a line of thousands of people, two abreast, quietly inching toward a large open window. It was a massive job fair for the industrial park. This seemingly endless ribbon of humanity was supplying labor to a park that was expanding seven miles in each direction each year and adding a new factory every four days. I reflected that only about 10 years ago, the Suzhou park had been a big rice paddy. Now it was a city of more than half a million people, a Chinese version of a gold rush town.

It has been said that the U.S. industrial revolution took one hundred years, the development of a modern economy in Japan took thirty years, and the equivalent level of change in China will take about fifteen years. Transforming the nation's "core" at the highest level, China found that its people, unshackled and unleashed, were the ultimate hidden asset. Given this pace of change, it is no wonder that the strategy cycles of the companies that fuel the world's economy are shortening.

I realized that more companies than ever were going to enter a period when their historic core was no longer enough, in its current state, to sustain profitable growth and that a fundamental strategic change was inevitable. Such change can be daunting for companies that have tens of thousands of employees, hundreds of products, serving millions of customers all over the world.

I began this research with a series of conversations with business executives, many of them, over a short period. Each echoed the same themes, though in very different industries—from personal computers to global logistics to retail to the newspaper business.

One such conversation went back and forth, thrust and parry, point and counterpoint until suddenly it stopped. A profound question hung in the air. It had been asked by Victor Fung, CEO and group chairman of Li & Fung, one of the leading supply-chain management companies in the world. Li & Fung is a symbol of the rise of modern China and an example of a company that has drawn on hidden assets to reinvent its core. I was speaking to Dr. Fung in his Hong Kong office overlooking an endless procession of cargo ships in the harbor below. It had struck me that the ships were like determined carpenter ants playing their assigned roles in reconstructing the world. We were talking about the challenges of fundamental change, and his question was this: "There is an old Chinese proverb: 'Sometimes to be reborn, you first must die.' In a world that is speeding up, how will companies change enough without crisis?"

I had no answer then for Dr. Fung. It wasn't until we examined the data for this book that we found the real key to redefinition: those hidden assets. And there is a lot of data. This book is based on the largest study I am aware of on the patterns and risks of making deep, fundamental change in a business's strategic direction. The main sources of information were as follows:

- A fifteen-year database tracking the performance of 8,400 companies in the G-7 economies.

- An examination of five hundred U.S. public companies from 1995 to 2004, focusing both on their financial performance and on changes that they made in their core.

- Analysis of the fifteen largest "big-bang" strategies announced and pursued by major corporations in the past ten years, along with a scorecard of current results.

- Two global surveys of business executives conducted with the Economist Intelligence Unit. One, titled Growth Survey, was conducted in October 2004; it asked 259 executives about the challenges and barriers to growth in their core business. The other, Capability Survey, took place in November 2005. This one asked 240 executives about their needs for new capabilities as part of a competitive strategy.

- In-depth case studies of twenty-five carefully selected companies around the world that have successfully confronted issues of core redefinition. This research included extensive in-person interviews with the CEOs and other members of the management teams.

The appendix describes our research methodology.

This book completes a trilogy of sorts on the topic of how companies define and grow their core (*Profit from the Core*) and push out their boundaries into new territory (*Beyond the Core*), only to one day discover that they need to redefine and renew their core (*Unstoppable*). I undertook this research at Bain & Company, where I am a leader of the Global Strategy Practice. What I failed to realize, early in the process, was how the "focus-expand-redefine" cycle of growth was accelerating. As a result, many more management teams will spend much more time than ever before confronting fundamental issues, even incipient crises, deep in their cores.

This book examines how companies can improve their ability to recognize the need to redefine their business model and lays out proven methods to improve the chances of successfully accomplishing this risky, but often essential, mission.

Unstoppable exists at the intersection of three bodies of work. The first is the literature on turnarounds, epitomized by *Good to Great*, by Jim Collins. That book focuses on management, leadership, and organization. *Unstoppable* examines the strategic dimension of performance renewal.

The second body of work that this book builds on is the search for growth opportunities in difficult and low-growth markets. *How to Grow When Markets Don't*, by Adrian J. Slywotsky and Richard Wise, is a key contribution. *Unstoppable* differs from that book in its examination not only of low-growth markets but also of the full range of situations when a strategy reaches a limit, fundamentals of the business are called into question, and the question is what to do next.

The third area that this book spans is strategic innovation. This work has two strands. One focuses on the critical importance of having a novel point of view of the future that you can translate into strategic changes, along with investments in the right new core capabilities, ahead of competitors. *Competing for the Future,* a 1994 book by Gary Hamel and C. K. Prahalad, is the business classic in examining this issue. The other stream of thought explores ways that companies can innovate within their core business model to find untapped markets—"white spaces" or "blue oceans," in some authors' lexicons. *Blue Ocean Strategy,* by W. Chan Kim and Renée Mauborgne, is a successful recent book that suggests one approach to find these untapped pockets of market opportunity. *Unstoppable* is different from this literature in its provision of empirical data on success rates of various possible paths, and most of all by its focus on the use of hidden assets to improve the odds and generate innovative new strategic alternatives. This book also offers a methodology for attacking the difficult issue of what to do when your past strategy starts to reach a limit. Because it connects to, and completes, a series of three books on the topic of sustained and profitable growth, it is unique in the breadth of the approach it recommends and the range of its demonstrated practical application by management teams.

A key, and somewhat surprising, finding is that the best blueprint for core renewal seldom requires leaps to distant and hot new markets, mandates being the first adopter of a pioneering new technology, or demands a "big-bang" acquisition. Rather, the most successful companies at redefining their core strategies use assets that they already have at hand or to which they have easy access. In our case studies, we found that pivotal assets often proved to have been hidden. Yet exploiting these hidden assets allowed these businesses, for a while, to move from unsustainable to unstoppable.

This book provides a simple framework for understanding how hidden assets can become the keys to transformation and identifies the best techniques for detecting and using them in your own business.

1

Unsustainable to Unstoppable

Diamonds. "Tears of the gods." The most concentrated form of wealth known to humanity. Few objects conjure such a range of experience and emotion. Searing heat in deep layers of the earth's mantle yields the product called *ice*. Miners in hardscrabble African villages and polishers in India's bustling diamond centers create gemstones worn by the world's elite. A product often associated with bleak and poor regions, diamonds have become a symbol of enduring love.

For all the emotions evoked by the gems and their production, the business world of diamonds was, for decades, more like diamond itself: colorless and highly stable. De Beers Consolidated Mines, descendant of a company founded in 1880 by explorer and adventurer Cecil Rhodes, reigned over the world's diamond supply, parceling out the gems to dealers in a manner designed to maintain prices and protect profits. Sir Ernest Oppenheimer, chairman of the company that controlled perhaps three-quarters of all diamonds mined and sold in the twentieth century, described the strategy explicitly: "Only by limiting the quantity of diamonds put on the market, in accordance with the demand, and by selling through one channel, can the stability of the diamond trade be maintained."[1]

Yet by 1999, De Beers's run of success, like all good things, seemed to have come to an end. New Chairman Nicky Oppenheimer and new Group Managing Director Gary Ralfe were looking at a company whose market value had declined substantially, whose market growth rate had turned negative, whose profit margins were hovering close to zero, and whose share of global production had dropped to around 40 percent. As Oppenheimer and Ralfe discussed the situation with shareholders, the other board members, outside analysts, and the management team, they found no shortage of opinions about how to tackle the situation.

Some observers felt that the market would turn around. It was thought that the key was to hold the course for a bit longer, cutting costs and using De Beers's industry scale to resuscitate the century-old formula of supply control. But hadn't things changed forever with the entrance of new competitors? Others believed that the answer was to attempt to recoup market share of production by acquiring competitors or by investing in new mines. Of course, De Beers was already investing in new mines. The question was, How would further investment revive the company's performance in a new competitive environment, where the development of synthetic diamonds was on the rise? Was it possible that De Beers's primary source of past differentiation as the controller of supply was finally reaching some natural limit?

One of De Beers's unique and most valuable assets was a $5 billion stockpile of rough diamonds that it could draw on to stabilize prices in the marketplace. Yet even this massive asset was no longer an effective tool, and it was becoming difficult to maintain given its enormous economic opportunity cost. A few mavericks suggested that perhaps De Beers should begin to diversify into new areas, recognizing that the market for diamonds was not what it used to be. But wasn't that the riskiest strategy of all? De Beers was diamonds.

As the financial pressure mounted, the management team concluded that the situation De Beers faced would not be reversed by following a strategy close to the one it had followed in the past.

Maybe, they thought, the answer could be found in De Beers's many underutilized customer assets: its unique image in consumers' eyes as the custodian of what the company would come to call "the diamond dream" as well as the strong De Beers brand, the company's unique access to and reputation with customers at all points in the value chain, and its track record as the provider of the most valued gems in the world. Perhaps the company could find a way to shift from a supply-based source of competitive differentiation to a new strategy built on these hidden assets.

And find a way it did. De Beers shifted the strategic focus from its obvious asset—the mines and the huge stockpile of rough diamonds—to hidden assets rooted in the company's unique relationship with consumers and customers and the power of the De Beers brand, which is virtually synonymous with the finest diamond gemstones. These assets and their power were hidden, because the success of the supply-driven strategy had long compelled a focus on the supply-based assets. This focus was intensified by the formal, almost secretive relationship De Beers had with its customers, who purchased gems in lots they could not view beforehand at what were essentially take-it-or-leave-it prices. Once the notion surfaced to turn the strategy on its head, ideas came fast and furiously, as if bottled up for years: branding, retail, jewelry design, consumer segmentation, and the umbrella marketing concept of De Beers as global custodian for all time of the diamond dream.

In the months that followed, De Beers outlined and began to implement this strategy, a radical departure from its profit model. The company liquidated 80 percent of its diamond inventory and invested in new forms of generating demand and in getting closer to each customer segment. It invested in brand building. It developed new product ideas for its distributors and jewelers and new consumer advertising campaigns to market those ideas. For example, De Beers developed the three-stone ring (to celebrate the past, present, and future of a relationship, or the birth of a child), diamond rings for men, and the "right hand" ring for women—a diamond ring women bought themselves as a symbol of independence.

For the first time in a century, De Beers even restructured its storied client base and uniquely strict contracts to sight-holders, its core customer base. Sight-holders are the diamond dealers and cutters and polishers who buy rough stones and turn them into gems for future sale. One observer, looking at De Beers's history and proposed future, queried in the midst of the change, "Can an ardent market manipulator such as De Beers, which until recently was proud to call itself The Syndicate, really be taken seriously when it announces such a dramatic volte face? After all, its first two changes alone will shine enough light on murky practices to revolutionize the gem trade . . . The new rules will change this relationship dramatically."[2] And they did.

Gareth Penny, the current group managing director, explains:

> It was clear when the senior team got together in 1999 that we had to make major changes. You have to start with the big questions: what is your DNA? What is it you are really good at? I think most people are not very good at understanding their core. In 1999 I am not sure that we understood that, or how it had changed.
>
> We have been more successful than we expected. Driving demand, we have gone from negative growth in diamond jewelry worldwide to over 3 percent growth per annum and, more recently, to over 5 percent growth. This is a significant accomplishment in a $60 billion global industry. By 2001, we valued the diamond part of the business at $9.3 billion, quite a change from its estimated value of only $1 billion just two years earlier. [De Beers contained more than the diamond business; for instance, it held a 35 percent stake in Anglo American, a diversified mining conglomerate.][3]

No two situations are alike, and De Beers is clearly a unique business with a history like none other. However, the wrenching issues faced by Oppenheimer, Ralfe, Penny, and the rest of the company's management team are not unusual. Are the changes in the marketplace ephemeral or permanent? Will they happen gradually, buying us time? Or are we at the tipping point of acceleration into crisis? Can the solution be found in operational restructuring or organizational change, through fundamental strategic redirection, or some combination of all three? If the answer is strategic, what is the right path forward? Is it a small course correction, or is it more significant? What do I do now? And how do I keep running a business while working at the same time to change it fundamentally?

This book is about what to do when you begin to fear that your success formula may be approaching (or careening toward) its natural limit or seems to be losing momentum. The focus of the research underlying the book was to distill the lessons of companies from around the world that set out to reinvigorate their businesses by making fundamental strategic changes. We set out to understand how businesses that seemed to be on an unsustainable path, and facing challenges that were becoming more difficult, reinvented their strategy, renewed their performance, and at the same time continued to operate. How did these management teams identify a new course? Which methods were most useful in figuring it out? What are the repeatable success factors that can be applied in other businesses? How did the companies shift from one course to another?

Jim Collins, in his book *Good to Great,* looked at the remarkable stories of eleven businesses that made significant and lasting improvements in their performance. But in *Unstoppable,* the focus is on strategic redirection. Collins's companies generally did not redefine their strategy but rather revitalized their organizations, management approaches, and operations. In addition, this book examines closely the role of hidden strategic assets in transformation, a topic not probed in *Good to Great.*

The intent is by no means to suggest that strategic change is always the answer. Often it is not. Nor is the objective to discover a silver bullet solution to a vexing problem. Instead, my goal is to provide some lenses and benchmarks and tools that executives can use when it begins to dawn on them that their company's core strategy and competitive advantage of the past may no longer be enough for the future.

The Death of the Long Term

More companies than ever are encountering the need to redefine their strategies as the world continues to speed up and industry turbulence becomes the norm and not the exception. An analysis that we conducted at Bain & Company indicated that in the 1970s only about 15 to 20 percent of industries could be defined as turbulent, with major changes in the rules for winning and rapid changes in how competitors positioned themselves versus each other. By contrast, now we estimate that as many as half of industries can be deemed to be turbulent by that definition, and there are few signs that this situation will end soon.

In business, the frequency with which management teams are encountering such inflection points in their business, where major strategic redirection is called for, is increasing. For instance, in our 2004 Growth Survey of 259 executives worldwide, 60 percent reported that their primary source of competitive advantage in their core business was eroding rapidly; 65 percent said that they would need to fundamentally restructure the commercial model they used to serve their core customers; and 72 percent believed that their primary competitor in five years would not be the company that was currently their primary competitor. This level of perceived competitive pressure is higher than we had seen before.

Our research team at Bain conducted an extensive analysis of the *Fortune* 500 over the past two decades, looking at the actual amount of change sought and achieved by these companies. We defined major change as making significant observable shifts in direction in the core business, restructuring the portfolio of a conglomerate, being acquired, or going into bankruptcy. In the decade from 1985 to 1994, some 49 percent of companies experienced this level of change; from 1995 to 2004, the proportion was 57 percent. We predict that this number will rise to 72 percent in the next decade (figure 1-1).

FIGURE 1-1

Rates of change in *Fortune* 500 companies

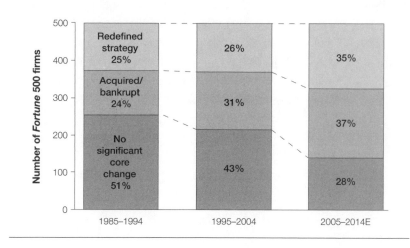

Remarkably, we found that 153 of the top 500 companies in 1994 did not even survive the following decade intact. They either ended up in bankruptcy (for example, WorldCom and Polaroid) or were acquired and integrated into a larger company. Of the 347 companies that survived and maintained independence, we judged that 130 had undergone a fundamental shift in their core business strategy and its key parameters. In other words, nearly six out of ten companies faced threats to their survival or independence, and only about half were able to meet those threats by redefining their strategies.

Nor were the failures mere stragglers; indeed, some ranked among the top twenty-five companies in the United States ten years ago as measured by return on equity. This group included Reebok, which was purchased in 2006 by Adidas after a decade of failed strategies, and AT&T, which was acquired by SBC, which kept the AT&T name. CBS was a turbulent story; it merged with Westinghouse, lost leadership quickly to CNN in news, combined with Viacom, and recently was spun off with Viacom's other broadcasting segments as a separate media company. Motorola is in recovery after failing at a foray into satellite phone services and losing leadership in the mobile-phone handset market to Nokia and, for a time, to Samsung.

What forces are accelerating the pace of business? The causes of this change are not the focus of this book; rather, we focus on what to do about them. Moreover, there is no shortage of well-researched books on the topic of global forces. However, it is probably worth taking a moment to list seven key trends that my team identifies as root causes for much of the turbulence observed in our case studies:

- Faster movement of information on everything from competitive moves to pricing to customer bids to know-how

- Increased rate at which large blocks of capital are mobilized and shifted

- Increasingly rapid movement of executives among companies, reducing barriers to competition

- The rise of China's and India's low-cost (and, in some cases, new) competitors, creating ripple effects in many industries

- Reduced capital intensity among the most profitable new industries, such as software and biotechnology, allowing them to morph and consolidate faster than industries of the past

- The rise of private equity firms and their ability to shake up entire industries

- Continued acceleration of technology innovation, reducing product cycle times

The supporting, and truly amazing, statistics on these topics could fill volumes. Let me cite a few that may be particularly important in the future. For instance, the percentage of global acquisitions made by private equity firms has increased in the past five years, from 3 percent of the total to 16 percent on the heels of 2005's fund-raising boom. In 2005, private equity firms raised more than

$170 billion in the United States alone; this amount was more than the total raised in the previous four years combined, and almost as much as in the history of the industry. These professional buyers are increasingly in search of industries where they can spur consolidation or take a leading company private to restructure it away from the jitters of impatient public markets.

The impatience of public markets, as well as the speed at which capital moves, is evident in the remarkable decline in the average holding period of a share of common stock. It has gone from eight years in the 1960s to three years in the 1980s to less than a year now. Hints of slowing growth or of burgeoning profit opportunities cause capital to move to the next hot area like quicksilver. This is a tough situation for executives to live in.

No wonder the average life span of companies is shortening. It has declined from about fourteen years to ten-to-twelve years, and it mirrors the declining length of tenure of CEOs (from about eight years a decade ago to less than five years now). No wonder more than 80 percent of the 259 global executives in our growth survey indicated that the cycle times of their strategies were shortening. Businesses are becoming increasingly unsustainable, multiplying the difficulty as well as the value of becoming unstoppable for a few more years.

Unsustainable to Unstoppable

The popular press on strategic renewal often emphasizes the spectacular. Longtime rivals Compaq and Hewlett-Packard combine to create a new $60 billion company to take on Dell, amid anguish from the founders and subsequently the dismissal of the CEO. Nokia undergoes metamorphosis from an industrial conglomerate whose best-known product line was rubber boots into a global telecommunications company. Samsung restructures its conglomerate, divesting itself of dozens of companies and reducing its workforce by one-third, and turns itself from a diverse company known for high variety and low quality into a quality leader focused on consumer electronics. In doing this, the company increases its market value from $2 billion in 1996 (when it was heading toward bankruptcy) to $78 billion in 2005 and becomes one of the most feared competitors in its industry.

Yet these sorts of cases, although boosting revenues, profits, and market capital when they are successful, are relatively rare and are not always the best places to look for universal lessons. The extreme points are interesting and are the starting point for many great insights in mathematics and physics, but in business they are not necessarily the place to begin crafting strategy.

Instead, we found that nearly all the successful and relatively lasting cases of renewal spring from existing assets in or near organizations' core businesses, assets that had been underappreciated and undervalued for their future potential. In twenty-one of our twenty-five case studies of successful strategic redefinition, a hidden asset was the linchpin for the new strategy.

Hidden Assets: The Key to Becoming Unstoppable

A hidden asset, as I refer to it in this book, is something that you possess whose value, properties, or potential you have not fully appreciated or realized. The more complicated, large, or established your company, the more likely it is that you possess numerous hidden assets, some of which might contain unmined veins of business gold.

Why are such valuable possessions hidden? There are many reasons. It could be that a change in market conditions has made an asset more valuable. Or it could be that you have not been at a stage in your strategy when you could take full advantage of it because of constrained resources. Or perhaps you have since acquired new capabilities that make the asset more valuable to you than it once was. Or it could be that you now see the asset in a new light. Examples of all these situations exist in the cases described in this book.

In a number of the stories here, the hidden asset was truly obscure, revealing itself only in the context of an all-out effort to develop the next-generation strategy and a search for sources of competitive differentiation on which to build it. Perhaps the most widely followed recent story of renewal is Apple Computer, which shifted its center of gravity toward the music business by drawing on design and software expertise resident in its computer business, adding to it new capabilities in online music software and digital rights management with record companies.

For many reasons, large and complex businesses seem to accumulate these assets over time and see them mostly in the context of their value in the past and not the future. As a result, they do not inventory, assess, or track these assets regularly, because they don't appear in the typical financials or charts of accounts. This is true of the value of a support service that has the potential to be a business in its own right, and of the full potential of subcore businesses. It's true of customer information and proprietary knowledge; and most particularly it is true of capabilities, such as R&D and supply chains and ongoing support services.

Maybe it's not surprising that assets we fail to track and measure are typically undervalued and often even unrecognized. Certainly, discovering even one of them is like finding a grand master painting gathering dust in a closet. The following example shows how assets literally in front of our eyes can hold profound, unrecognized value.

Marvel Entertainment: Hidden Powers from Superheroes

Storybook characters who are suddenly imbued with special powers and accomplish amazing feats captivate us in our youth, inhabiting our imaginations. There is something both fascinating and hopeful in the possibility of becoming dramatically more powerful than we are, even superhuman.

Spider-Man was a nerdy high school student who suddenly was able to scale walls, create and swing on super-strong web threads, and sense danger acutely. He came into these singular skills when he was bitten by a radioactive spider. In adventure after adventure, Spider-Man battles supervillains that mortals could not hope to compete with, such as Green Goblin, an evil businessman who developed superhuman abilities after exposure to an experimental serum.

Almost all the Marvel heroes follow this formula: beings somehow transformed through outside forces, gaining new and astounding powers. As if life were imitating art, the company that created and controlled this stable of superheroes underwent its own renewal, changing its form almost as amazingly as Spider-Man.

In 1996, Marvel was in bankruptcy, its voluminous library of comic-book characters not worth enough to stave off creditors. But then Marvel got new leadership: director Isaac Perlmutter (who eventually became CEO in 2005) and creative leader Avi Arad. After a time, the two saw a way to change the company's strategy dramatically. They saw their asset with the highest potential for renewing the business not as a comic-book franchise but as a stable of great characters, more than five thousand of them, to which former readers of comic books felt a strong nostalgic attachment. They decided to work with film studios to turn Marvel's popular characters into movie stars. It worked. Spider-Man led the way, followed soon after by his brethren, such as Wolverine, and the Incredible Hulk. By 2005, revenues from character licensing for movies and merchandise accounted for more than half of Marvel's $390 million in revenues and much of its $103 million in profits.

The story of Marvel Entertainment is impressive in the magnitude of the change. Yet it is especially noteworthy in how the company built the new strategy on hidden assets—the library of characters and stories that had been underused and undervalued. Even though few other companies can call on an army of allies as unique as Spider-Man, Wolverine, and the Hulk, the basic need that Marvel confronted—a core business that was approaching a limit of growth—was not unique.

Paths to Redefine Your Core

The revivals of De Beers and Marvel Entertainment have common elements. Both companies experienced basic changes in their industries—changes that were closing the book on strategies that had been successful for decades. Both were proud companies whose economics were in rapid decline. Both faced a range of possible options, from combining with competitors to defending the status quo to investing available resources to leap to a hot market. And both found the answer in underutilized, latent assets, and in strategies that were organic (as opposed to discontinuous leaps).

Each seemed stopped in its tracks, unsustainable; yet each proved not to be stopped, at least not at that time and by those forces.

This book focuses on this practical pattern of successful redefinition. But other paths are often tempting when the pressure is on and the best answer is not apparent. Organizations can defend the status quo even under extreme changes in the industry, can take what resources they have left and put them into the best hot market they can find, or can attempt a big-bang acquisition or a series of large transforming moves.

Defending the Status Quo

One possible route to take when the competitive battleground around you is changing is to defend the status quo in hopes that you have a niche position that can be protected or in hopes that everyone else is wrong. Certainly, the size of a potential change can be overestimated. We saw that kind of overestimation during the years of the Internet bubble, when, for instance, there were endless pronouncements about how the "clicks" of the Internet would rapidly make the "bricks" of legacy businesses, such as retail, obsolete. Clearly, this happened to a much lesser extent than many pundits forecast. More than 99 percent of Internet start-ups in that period went out of business within three years after the bubble burst, and it was the old economy companies that often snapped up the Internet technology for themselves.

However, when the entire technology base of an established industry shifts (such as from analog to digital) or the rules of competition change fundamentally (such as in mass retailing), those who fail to change can rapidly fall far behind. We identified sixteen industries that satisfied these conditions of rapid and fundamental change, and we followed the fortunes of the major participants. We found that companies that defended the status quo under these conditions earned far lower returns, on average, than companies that did not. In some cases, the defender of the old model seemed to choose the status quo deliberately (Borders in books, perhaps); in other cases, the defender of the past seemed unable to act (Polaroid in photography). But change can happen fast. For example, just five years ago one analyst proclaimed Sun Microsystems "clearly the Internet infrastructure leader" as its stock rose to more than $60 per share adjusted for revenues and splits. Five years later, the stock was selling at less than $4, with 80 percent of the decline coming soon after this peak pronouncement.

Big-Bang Transforming Moves

In January 2000, the $150 billion takeover of media giant Time Warner by Internet portal America Online was announced to great fanfare just as the Internet bubble was about to burst. Analysts and journalists alike seemed to be awestruck by this potentially transforming move. One publication, rarely noted for breathlessness, put the deal on the cover and referred to it in the first paragraph of the article as "one of those events that have the potential to change the competitive landscape so fundamentally that nothing can be the same again."[4] Yet now the companies are moving apart again, the combination proving to have been less, and not more, than the sum of the parts. Who could have known?

Redefining strategies are rarely created through big-bang transforming moves like AOL's merger with Time Warner, and when they are, the odds of success are low. Similar examples include McKesson's move from drug distribution to medical information technology with the purchase of HBO & Co.; luxury leader LVMH's move into retail with the purchase of the DFS group of duty free stores; and AT&T's acquisitions in cable television and purchase of McCaw Cellular.

We studied these strategies systematically by identifying fifteen of the most heralded big-bang transformations of the past ten years. We compiled that list by screening news stories of major business transformations, eliminating strategies that were simply industry consolidation and not fundamental change in scope or business model. Most of these big bangs included one or more large acquisitions, often accompanied by internal restructurings and organic growth initiatives to supplement the larger moves.

Our analysis of the results of these strategies was sobering. None of the fifteen companies increased its market value over the period by more than the average of the stock market. In fact, eleven of the fifteen companies experienced a decline in market value, and seven of them declined in value by more than 50 percent. As a comparison, we examined a control group of over 2,000 companies more than $500 million in size in the G-7 economies from 1990 to 2002, and we found that only 30 percent of public companies (those that were still in existence) declined in market value by more than 50 percent. That's still a somewhat surprisingly large number; but in comparison, nearly half of the big-bang strategists had seen their value decline more than 50 percent. We also looked at the results relative to an index of other companies in the same industry and found essentially the same thing: only about 30 percent of companies within the same industry declined in market value by more than 50 percent.

What accounts for this difference? Clearly, each circumstance involves a detailed explanation and set of factors. In fact, it's possible in a few cases to argue that the company would have been worse off had it not made a large move, even if market values did not reflect it. But when we looked case by case at the causes identified by analysts and industry observers, it became clear that the companies faced common challenges. Large, complex problems in a core business can seldom be solved by single, large moves. Often, large moves are the result of waiting too long and lurching into a big action.

Furthermore, it is much harder and more complex to execute a large move than to take a gradual approach to transformation using hidden assets—if such an alternative path can be found in time.

The Cold Truth of Hot Markets

Perhaps another version of a big-bang transforming move is the decision to shift the center of gravity of the company to a new, hot market, diversifying away from the current core business. This strategy is a great temptation for companies that seem to be stuck in low-growth industries or whose positions seem untenable or that are simply bored with their core business. In reality, the odds of success of big-bang moves in creating profitable growth in revenue and stock are significantly less than 10 percent. Meanwhile, the odds are much better for moves to new growth platforms that are only one step away from a strong core (they involve expansion into, say, a new customer segment, distribution channel, or step in the value chain only one step away from the company's current business) and that build on the company's existing knowledge and assets. These moves have a success rate of at least 30 to 40 percent.

Jumping four to five steps away from your core is like playing the lottery, a growth strategy that amounts to no more than a wild bet.[5] We have seen this over the years in hundreds of cases, despite the evidence on the risk: Vivendi moving from water into entertainment; Motorola moving from engineering products into wireless services; Corning moving from kitchenware into fiber optics. The list goes on and on.

For instance, in the early 1990s Grupo Pulsar was a highly successful Mexican conglomerate that had experienced five years of 26 percent growth and had increased profit margins eightfold via its holdings in insurance and in tobacco products. Wishing to diversify to even faster growth industries, the company followed a strategy, executed in rapid fire, to enter and consolidate the market for bio-engineered seeds. The result was a disaster. The stock price dove from

$4.50 a share in early 2000 to almost zero by the end of that year as the company missed bank covenant after bank covenant and careened out of control. What remained was eventually purchased by Monsanto. A once growing and profitable business had been traded for a ticket to disaster.

This does not mean that companies should not make opportunistic small bets along the way as unique opportunities or insights appear. In fact, it is essential to plant the seeds for the future and learn about opportunities. Nor does it mean that it is wrong to shift a core from one market to another. Some of the key examples in this book, such as the transformation of PerkinElmer, involve such a shift. But it's a loser's game to make "bet the company" plans based on studying a hot market. This is especially the case if there is a way to redefine your core business more gradually by shifting your center of gravity along an existing proven vector of growth, using assets that you possess and have mastered but have not fully exploited, or transforming the *way* you do business with a highly focused acquisition of new capabilities.

Usually, redefinition is not about finding a new, hot market but rather finding a more viable and repeatable formula for growth. *Blue Ocean Strategy,* by W. Chan Kim and Renée Mauborgne, describes a method that can be used to detect unserved markets or new, emerging markets. These authors' approach can be used to identify profitable new growth opportunities. This strategy is related to, but different from, the topic we address here: the adaptation of an existing business to fundamentally new conditions in the future, rather than the pure search for new growth and innovative ideas about untapped markets.

The Odds of Success of a Strategic Redefinition

The odds of success, based on our research and an extensive review of the literature, are described and developed throughout this book.

The odds vary greatly based on your company's circumstances: the strength of your business and the dynamics of your specific industry, as well as how you choose to measure success. However, the odds for the extreme strategies of big bangs, major diversifications, and holding on to the status quo despite changes in industry rules are remarkably consistent across most situations and research angles—and all are extremely low. Yet each path offers its unique temptation, like the narrow opening in the trees to a distant green when your golf shot ends up in the woods, beckoning you away from a safer route. The hot market beckons with its promise of growth and the chance you might be the winner. The big-bang move tempts with the decisive nature of bold action. The status quo offers false safety—temporary shelter from the storm. But what if the storm never ends?

Some of the worst odds, less than 10 percent success, come from doggedly defending the status quo when your markets have turned turbulent and the competitor and customer dynamics are altering the basic rules of competition. It is possible to play to be the "last man standing" or to retreat to a niche that you can defend for a while. However, it is rare to see your entire industry change around you and avoid redefining yourself. Our data here comes primarily from analysis of sixteen turbulent industries and the fates of the companies that followed various paths. The odds are also quite poor from undertaking a big-bang transforming move, such as the AOL/Time Warner acquisition—about 5 to 10 percent chance of success at best. The odds of leaping to a new, hot market (as Vivendi tried to do) are not much better—about 10 to 15 percent.

The low odds of transforming by jumping into a new, hot market full force do not mean that the riskier paths are not appropriate, but it does mean that it is critical to understand the odds and to work hard to ensure that you are aware of the full range of options. Indeed, the lower-risk paths opened up by hidden assets, although often the best route, can also be the most difficult to follow in the thicket of confusion that often characterizes turbulent industry environments. The tragedy would be to follow the less attractive paths simply because they are more obvious.

Raising the Odds Through Hidden Assets

In the award-winning movie *Apollo 13,* the crew discovers that it is losing its air supply while in a capsule in outer space and calls ground control with the memorable understatement, "Houston, we have a problem." A roomful of scientists convenes on the ground to figure out what to do. They quickly ask for a complete inventory of everything in the spacecraft, from underwear to chewing gum to duct tape. From these humble objects the answer emerges, a solution is developed, and the crew is saved and brought back to Earth. That the movie was based on the actual experience of American astronauts makes the story especially compelling.

The cases examined in this book illustrate the preferred route to safety and growth using the "humble objects" of the business in question, possibly seen in a different light or at least with a different urgency. When available, such solutions, based on the assets you already have access to, have a rate of success that is four to six times as high as the three other general paths just discussed.

Specifically, three types of hidden assets emerged as keys to the strategic renewals in our case studies (figure 1-2). Chapters 3, 4, and 5 examine each of these in turn:

- Undervalued business platforms

- Unexploited customer assets

- Underutilized capabilities

FIGURE 1-2

Hidden assets in redefinition

Platforms	Customer assets	Capabilities
• Undeveloped adjacencies • Support organizations to the core • Noncore businesses and orphan products	• Unrecognized segments • Privileged access or trust • Underused data and information	• Hidden corporate capabilities • Noncore capabilities in the businesses • Underleveraged core capabilities in the businesses

Undervalued Business Platforms

Undervalued business platforms are parts of your business that might once have been secondary in importance but now have the potential to be the foundation for a new major core business. Usually these types of hidden assets take one of three primary forms. The first are business islands: small subcore businesses that have never been fully developed or a family of orphan products never invested in with a focused strategy.

Second are adjacent expansions that have been incidental to growth (for example, movement into new geographies, customer segments, steps in the value chain, or channels of distribution) but now have mass and power and uniqueness in their own right.

The third kind of undervalued business platform is an internal support function to the core that can become world class and broader in its reach. For instance, the remarkable rejuvenation of IBM in the past decade was built on a small-services business that had always been in the background of the hardware business. The transformation of PerkinElmer, described extensively in chapter 3, was designed around a life sciences product line scattered throughout its catalog of scientific instruments.

Unexploited Customer Assets

Unexploited customer assets come in three primary forms. The first is knowledge gathered as part of serving the customer but that, over time, accumulates an inherently greater value of its own. The renewal of American Express took hold when the company focused on a unique asset: the power of its payments network to provide insights about what customers and merchants wanted and how to deliver it to them.

The second form of hidden customer asset comes from a unique position of trust or relationship you have with a set of customers, giving you much more access and influence than has been recognized. De Beers is an example of a transformation built on a company's unexploited brand power and reputation with consumers.

The final type of customer asset comes in the form of hidden segments of customers that emerge when companies use new methods to disaggregate their customer base. These new segments have needs that often can be served best by a new, more focused business model. Although it is a work in process, Nike's ability to produce, economically, a line of shoes tailored to a particular microsegment—as it did for the Mister Cartoon line of tattooed Leather Cortez shoes for urban trendsetters—is a case in point. Further, if Nike's capabilities— its supply chain and design shop—allow it to target microsegments profitably, its combination of customer insight and capabilities to serve new customer segments gives it a marketing and production edge on competitors that changes the playing field for shoes.

Underutilized Capabilities

Underutilized capabilities are probably the most difficult hidden asset to discern but no less powerful. Most market leaders that lose position to attackers do so because of a growing capability gap in cost, speed, logistics, design, or the ability to deliver flawlessly to a customer. At the roots of such competitive reversals we often find a yawning capability gap that was undetected, dismissed, or ignored.

Similarly, in some of our case studies, companies that managed to upset competitors had built their new and redefined strategy on a capability that they had but did not use or had failed to fully develop. For instance, the remarkable turnaround of Autodesk, the leader in software for computer-aided design, was built in part on next-generation modeling and 3-D graphics superiority that helped the company drive deep into vertical market segments in ways that outflanked its competitors.

Success Rates

The odds of success, based on our analysis and other studies of business transformation, are shown in figure 1-3. What is striking is the large gap between an organic approach using hidden assets, where such a path can be found, and the alternative paths of defending the status quo as the world around you changes, diversifying rapidly to a hot new market, or attempting a big-bang move. The approaches using hidden assets worked to improve returns and drive new growth about one-third of the time, whereas the other approaches had success rates that hovered closer to one in ten.

In all these cases, the insight about hidden assets came about through a combination of luck (that the assets were there), vision (having an idea of what the company hoped to do in the future), logic (a framework to think systematically about the business and its potential economics), and intuition or lateral thinking. Throughout this book, I highlight approaches you can take to increase the odds of recognizing the value of your hidden assets. Hopefully, this will help you see your business in new ways, as if you were putting on polarizing sunglasses that allow you to see

FIGURE 1-3

Success rates of different strategies when rules of the core change

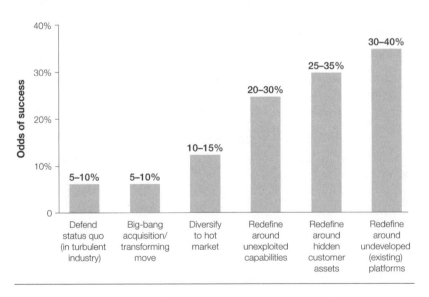

through the water's glare to recognize patterns that you had not appreciated before.

Of course, there are impossible cases, where a business model is so outmoded that no breakthrough or renewal is possible. In those cases the answer may be to combine with another company, to shrink to a small part of your business that is sustainable, or even to exit. However difficult such moves may be, the greater tragedy would be to have the elements of victory at hand and to cede defeat.

This book does four things to help executives who face the prospect of redefining their strategies. First, it offers evidence on the odds of success of the primary pathways that we have seen companies follow, recognizing that not all companies find a path to renewal. Many stagnate for a while, or exit, or sell to competitors.

Second, it identifies, with examples, definitions, and statistics, the primary types of hidden assets that we found were most valuable in defining and implementing positive change.

Third, the book provides a series of case examples, often in the words of the executives themselves. Each case embodies specific lessons and insights of its own for others who face similar challenges. Finally, the book offers specific frameworks and ideas for detecting hidden assets and for exploring whether they can be important ingredients in the renewal of your core.

Steps to Core Renewal

Management teams must take certain steps to judge whether it is time to redefine and to decide how and when to do it. Although these steps can be taken in parallel, there is a natural sequence. (See the box "Seven Steps to Redefining Your Core".) Companies that get into trouble or lurch into big-bang moves often realize, too late, that they did not follow a methodical process nor build their strategies on facts and consensus.

Seven Steps to Redefining Your Core

The redefinition process that we find works most often, and forms the basis for the architecture that underlies this book, is the following:

1. *Develop a point of view on impending turbulence* in your industry and the speed at which change will happen (see chapter 2). The key indicator is the current and expected distribution of profitability across markets, business models, substitutes, and steps in the value chain in your industry. The unifying framework for thinking about turbulence is the focus-expand-redefine cycle (FER cycle) of business and the shift of industry profit pools that are defined and discussed in chapter 2.

2. *Evaluate the "state of the core" in your business,* focusing particularly on what might happen to your source of competitive differentiation in serving your core customers (see chapter 2 for a diagnostic approach) in light of the trends identified.

3. *Identify a first set of options* for a new point of arrival given the point of departure that you have just characterized. Strategy under turbulence usually presents a business with a set of discrete, distinct options (versus incremental variations of the same thing).

4. *X-ray your organization for hidden assets* that might create new options, refine current options, or improve your ability to implement on those options. These hidden assets—what they are and how to find them—is the subject of chapters 3, 4, and 5.

5. *Refine your set of options* based on what you've learned about hidden assets and continue to iterate between steps

3, 4, and 5 until you believe you've fully developed and understood the strategic choices that you face with regard to redefining your core strategy.

6. *Evaluate the options with clear, agreed-upon criteria:* The most important ingredients to such evaluation, we find, are the ability to be truly differentiated in a set of core customers and to protect that position competitively, the ability to add the new capabilities that are required for the redefined strategy, and the organization's ability to implement. Our research shows that companies embarking on a new strategy often need to go through a period of operational restructuring to tighten up the organization and to render it "battle ready" for the pace of change, and the resources required.

7. *Enter the mobilization phase with full force.* Some of the key elements of mobilization are discussed in chapter 6, though this is not a book about the details of change management. Three areas to focus on in particular are: (1) maintaining intensely high levels of clear communication and building consensus all the way to the front lines; (2) establishing a mechanism to measure progress in real time, to learn and to make course corrections; and (3) creating a program office at the center to monitor progress, provide help, and work on problems.

The rest of this book focuses on determining when it is necessary to redefine your core or its strategy (chapter 2) and on the roles of the three types of hidden assets in doing so (chapters 3–5). Its ultimate purpose is to provide a unifying framework as well as practical tools and methods for you to use in making your company unstoppable.

2

When to Redefine the Core

One of the most difficult decisions a CEO can face is whether to remain maniacally focused on extracting the full potential from the historic core or to begin the search for a new vein to mine—or a new approach to mining altogether. The escalating forces of change described in chapter 1 (increasing turbulence, speed, and the shortening shelf life of a strategy) make this choice both more commonly encountered and more difficult to act upon. CEOs must cope with a wider and more confusing array of choices, less job security and tenure to develop and execute a new plan, increasingly impatient and short-term-oriented investors, and a greater cost of being wrong.

Today this crisis of the core confronts some of the largest and most complex companies in sectors like telecommunications, media, airlines, automobiles, semiconductors, computers, software, and energy. Recently, the CEO of Ford, the fifth-largest corporation in America, sent a remarkable memo around to all employees saying, "The business model that sustained us for decades is no longer sufficient to ensure profitability."[1] On the other end of the spectrum, a similar choice also faces many smaller companies that were borne of a single, powerful core idea and are now trying to figure out how to adapt and sustain momentum as they grow. Examples would be Google in search engines or Amazon.com in book retailing.

So, when should you take on the risk and expense and distraction to adapt—or even prepare to abandon—your business model? When should you avoid distractions and drive for focus? And given the high cost of being wrong—how can you know?

Where Are You on the Cycle of Sustainable Growth?

Many human and natural phenomena follow cycles that allow us to chart them, understand them, and even predict them—the seasons, business cycles, the phases of the moon, the circle of life, the ages of man, human biorhythms. From ancient times until now, we use cyclical patterns to explain and organize much of our lives. Such cyclical and recurring patterns also exist in the rise and fall of human organizations, including businesses.

Our seven-year study of profitable growth reveals that sustainable-growth companies often exhibit a cyclical pattern over time. You can chart their shifts in focus from a preoccupation with strengthening their core, to exploring adjacent expansion moves at the boundaries of the core, to redefining the core and its fundamental capabilities. We refer to this as the focus-expand-redefine (FER) cycle of business (figure 2-1). Companies that make their way successfully through the entire cycle, in a sense, create the opportunity to restart the game through focus on a renewed core and economic model. The truth is, however, that three-quarters do not. Either they are defeated in the early stages of the business, they overexpand, or they expand successfully but are never able to redefine.

Establishing your company's coordinates on the FER cycle is step one when it comes to making correct and well-timed decisions that improve your odds of renewing or sustaining profitable growth.

Not all businesses experience every phase of the cycle during their lifetime. Some businesses never leave the focus phase, where they concentrate their energy on obtaining full potential from the core business within its current boundaries. Others oscillate between focus and expansion, where the center of attention shifts to growth initiatives that take advantage of existing capabilities and market

FIGURE 2-1

Focus-Expand-Redefine cycle

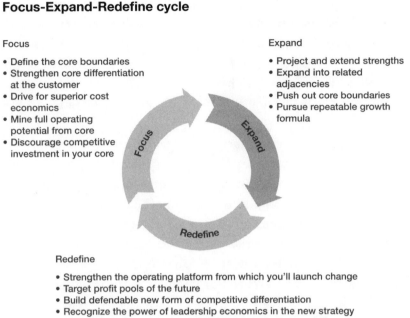

Focus

- Define the core boundaries
- Strengthen core differentiation at the customer
- Drive for superior cost economics
- Mine full operating potential from core
- Discourage competitive investment in your core

Expand

- Project and extend strengths
- Expand into related adjacencies
- Push out core boundaries
- Pursue repeatable growth formula

Redefine

- Strengthen the operating platform from which you'll launch change
- Target profit pools of the future
- Build defendable new form of competitive differentiation
- Recognize the power of leadership economics in the new strategy
- Heavily invest in required capabilities and capacity to mobilize

positions in the core, always making minor improvements and seeing adjacent opportunities one at a time. Still others live the full cycle as a matter of survival and routine, including redefinition, which calls for companies to focus on structural changes in the business model, the addition of significant new capabilities that transform the potential of the core, or possibly a shift to a different core.

For example, until January 2006, Kongo Gumi of Japan was the world's oldest known company. It arguably had not moved far beyond the focus phase for nearly millennium and a half. Kongo Gumi was founded in AD 578 to construct Buddhist temples, Shinto shrines, and castles in Japan. The company built the famous pagoda of the Shitennoji Temple and, over the centuries, had rebuilt it seven times after fires and wars—perhaps one of the oldest customer and supplier relationships in history. In fact, one of the principles articulated by the company was, "Don't leave your doors wide open"—meaning, "Focus on your core and do not diversify."[2]

Only recently did the company expand into surrounding adjacencies by constructing apartment and office buildings—a move that ultimately brought trouble, when debt from its real estate investments forced it into liquidation. Since then, the title for business longevity has passed to another Japanese firm, an inn called *Hoshi Ryokan,* which has stuck to its hospitality focus since its founding in 717—and is now being run by the forty-sixth generation of the Hoshi family.

Hoshi Ryokan is a member of the Henokiens, an association of the oldest family companies. In discussions I held with the association about the composition of its members and the reasons some businesses last for a long time, it became clear that many of these businesses had not gone through the full FER cycle. They had somehow avoided the extreme risks at the boundaries of the phases that most companies today will have to cycle through at least every decade in order to survive and prosper. Most of the oldest companies were in narrow niche businesses such as glass blowing, specialized sweets (e.g., licorice), bell foundry, cookware, or even hook manufacturing. In the United States, the same is true. The oldest U.S. company is the Zildjian Cymbal Co. of Norwell, Massachusetts. Zildjian, a transplant to American soil, traces its roots back fourteen generations to Constantinople. There, it was founded by an alchemist who had discovered a metal alloy that had unique musical properties perfect for manufacturing cymbals. In fact, *Zildjian* is the Armenian word for son of a cymbal maker.

But most companies are not like this. The environment forces change, creates opportunity, or spawns competitors that must be confronted. In fact, the average age of companies is declining. Fewer of them can avoid the task of periodically redefining their core.

It's fascinating to study long-lived businesses. But they are the business equivalent of the bony-finned coelacanth, discovered in 1938. It was thought to have been extinct but had been living in a static deep underwater environment for 400 million years. The natural world also contains powerful examples at the other extreme—turbulent, sudden change, which is more like the current business environment. For example, scientists have calculated that the extinction rate of species is now a thousand to ten thousand times what it has been through most of time. They attribute this rate to the rapid environmental changes on the planet, which currently cause fifty thousand species to become extinct each year. As Charles Darwin pointed out in *On the Origin of Species*, it is not the strongest that survive, but the most adaptable to the environment. The same can be said of businesses in many industries.

The Growth Cycle in Newspapers: The *New York Times*

Consider the turbulent newspaper industry and the FER stage currently faced by the *New York Times,* the best-known newspaper franchise in the world. From its origins as a broadsheet in 1851, the *Times* grew by intensely focusing on its core as a regional newspaper. By 1993, it was earning $2 billion in revenues and seeing operating profits of $126 million. But the company seemed to reach a natural limit. Revenue growth for the preceding decade averaged less than 3 percent per year; earnings had declined over the period, and the stock price had underperformed Standard & Poor's by a wide margin.

The answer for the next decade was a dramatic move beyond the New York metro area in circulation and advertising. The company turned the *Times* into a national newspaper by developing new channels of distribution outside New York, new segments of readership (which it then appealed to with different content), and new geographic markets. The shift to a national newspaper, perhaps an example of moving from a preoccupation with the core to an expansion of the core, was a rousing success. In ten years, revenues grew from $2 billion to $3.2 billion; operating profits more than quadrupled to $539 million; and the company's market value exploded from $2 billion to $8 billion. The company used the cash flow to extend its formula by purchasing strong regional newspapers like the *Boston Globe.*

Enter the Internet, new competitors, and online information. The paid aggregation of content that was the raison d'être of newspapers began to give way to the nearly free disaggregation of content, such as stock quotes on Yahoo!, classifieds on Monster.com, or instant headlines on CNN. But what now? Since its $8 billion peak, the company's market value has declined by nearly two-thirds as the world awaits the answer to the crisis of the core, not only for the *Times* but also for newspapers in general.

The *New York Times* is now confronting the redefine phase of the cycle in its industry and in its particular business—and realizes it acutely.

How the FER Cycle Shapes Strategic Priorities

A different set of strategic principles becomes paramount during each stage of the FER cycle, because organizations can (and should) focus on only a limited number of objectives at one time.

During the focus phase of the cycle, the rate of profitable growth in revenue and share price is heavily influenced by your company's ability to do three things: (1) rigorously define your core business and understand how it is different from your competitors', (2) consistently lower your cost position versus your key competitors, and (3) actively work to discourage your competitors from reinvesting in your core.

The first rule of strategy is to induce competitors to stop investing in your core. You influence that willingness by the strength of your differentiation, by your relative cost position, and by your ability and intent to match their investments.

If you come close to this Platonic ideal of business, you are almost assured of success during the focus phase of the cycle. For instance, in salty snacks, Frito-Lay has driven competitors away while continuously improving on cost, market share, and return on investment. Tetra Pak has done the same thing in sterile ambient beverage containers (such as milk and juice boxes), as has Enterprise Rent-A-Car in the insurance replacement-vehicle segment of the market, where it has attained overwhelming leadership.

However, even for relatively new businesses that are slugging it out with competitors in an evolving market—like automobile navigation systems with TomTom—the key to success in the focus phase comes down to these three principles.

During the expansion part of the cycle, a company builds on the economic strength of its core business, usually to extend and project its strengths to conquer other adjacent territory (such as new geographies, different customer segments, or new channels of distribution).

The three principles of shaping, focusing, and strengthening the core still apply. But three new strategic imperatives emerge and loom larger on the agenda: (1) pursue the power of a repeatable formula for adjacency expansion, (2) invest in the ability to attain superior customer insight (the key to successful adjacency expansion), and (3) recognize the speed at which adjacency success rates decline with distance from the core.

I examined the concept of economic distance from the core in the book *Beyond the Core* using a simple formula based on the number of major variables that are changing (customers, competitors, infrastructure, channel, etc.). We found that as soon as two variables were changing at a time (you were moving two steps away from your core), the odds of success began to plummet. It's almost as if complexity and a lack of knowledge increase exponentially with the number of major steps from the core.

The earlier example of the growth of the *New York Times* in the 1990s is such a case: an adjacency expansion for about a ten-year period. Nike's rise over Reebok (a company with which it was once neck-in-neck), achieved through Nike's repeatable formula, which allowed it to expand relentlessly from one sport into another, is another classic example of success through adjacency expansion.

When the need to redefine the historic core (or begin to shift to a new one) looms, a third cluster of strategic principles becomes paramount: (1) pursue the profit pool of the future and not the market of the future, (2) build the strategy in pursuit of differentiation and leadership, and (3) always invest in capabilities ahead of the curve.

When to Redefine Your Core

A few situations are almost always found at the roots of redefinition. In every one of our twenty-five case studies, the management team faced one or more of these troubling dilemmas:

- A shrinking or shifting of the future profit pool

- A direct threat to the core from a new competitive model or disruptive technology

- A stall-out in the growth formula and an erosion of differentiation

This section briefly examines each of these and suggests an approach to understanding the situation using what we call *the state of the core diagnostic.*

Situation 1: Shrinking or Shifting of the Future Profit Pool

Businesses thrive by earning profits. When profits dwindle or shift away from your core market, decay can set in, first consuming noncore activities and businesses and eventually affecting the ability to reinvest and to retain the best people. If Apple Computer had not shifted the center of its business toward digital music, one wonders about its ability to sustain its personal computer business, whose share had plummeted to less than 3 percent in a market where the profit pool was contracting. If Marvel had not turned its comic-book heroes into film stars, it would have found itself on an ever smaller island, eaten away each year by the natural erosion of its comic-book customer base. If IBM had not shifted its profit source toward services, it would have faced an untenable position in a shrinking profit pool around computer hardware.

A profit pool is different from a market.[3] A market is the mix and volume of products sold, not the business economics of those products. The profit pool for a market consists of the earnings of each participant in that market, from the beginning of the value chain (raw materials) to the end user.

There are many ways to measure the profit pool. You can calculate the sum of operating profits; all profits beyond the cost of capital; current profits and an estimate of future profits; or even creation of stock market value. All are ways to define whether a market can sustain a business, plus its need for reinvestments, plus its need for a reasonable return.

Measuring a profit pool is very different from measuring a market, and yet most people measure the market, not the profit pool, because market size and share are the information available in standard research reports. But when it comes to redefining your core, you can make major mistakes by focusing only on the market, without a parallel point of view on how the underlying profit pools are likely to evolve.

The key indicator of turbulence (as defined in this book) in an industry or market is a shift in the size or the location of the profit pool. There are several ways a profit pool can shift. It can collapse across the board, creating stress and chaos across many competitors (as happened in the airline industry after U.S. deregulation). It can shift dramatically among participants because of a new economic model (as when upstart Dell captured the vast majority of the profit pool in personal computers, even though it was not the industry market-share leader until late 1999). The profit pool's distribution across steps of the value chain (the activities that cause a product to move from raw inputs to final usage and disposal by the end consumer) can also shift, as in the case of De Beers, where influence over the profit pool shifted closer to the consumer, making activities like marketing, branding, and demand generation at retail much more valuable. Or, the profit pool can shift among totally different, but competing, products vying for customer attention. (An example would be the distribution of the profit pool in the consumer photography business, which has shifted from analog to digital products, creating enormous turbulence for some incumbents.) The onset of industry turbulence, we have found, usually hits harder and faster than most industry participants expected.

Take the market for photography as an example of how fast things can shift. The total profits earned in the photographic product and processing industry (from camera manufacturing to recording medium to photo finishing) actually grew substantially in the past ten years, from $1.9 billion in 1995 to $3.4 billion in 2005. On the surface, this would seem like a good thing for companies in the business in 1995. Yet, that is not universally true. The location of those profits has shifted nearly completely. Business activities such as film manufacturing, photo developing, and nondigital cameras, which once accounted for nearly all of the profit pool in the market, now account for much less than 20 percent. Past pockets of profit have collapsed, disappeared, or morphed into new areas like flash memory cards and online services. The impact on the competitors was powerful and varied, ranging from the bankruptcy of Polaroid, to the successful adaptation of Canon to digital technology, to the emergence of SanDisk in flash memory cards as leader in one of the strongest profit pools. Turbulence hits fast and can rearrange the profit pool in a flash.

General Dynamics: The Power of Perceiving Profit Pool Shifts. A classic case in which a company perceived a major profit pool collapse and acted ahead of its competitors is that of General Dynamics. This defense contractor has been the best-performing major company in its industry for more than a decade. Its success traces, in part, to one moment of insight. In 1984, nearing the end of the cold war, General Dynamics was the largest defense company in the United States, with revenues of $7.8 billion and 10 percent of Department of Defense procurement. With the stand-down in defense-force levels, the Department of Defense cut procurement significantly, from $128 billion at the peak in 1986 to a low point of $49 billion in 1996.

In the early 1990s General Dynamics commissioned a major study of demand and its asset values for every sector in which it participated. The company concluded that defense spending would fall throughout the decade and that it could make more money by selling many of its businesses than by retaining and operating them with low demand and low profits. In one of the most rapid and decisive corporate makeovers, the company sold most of its businesses, preempting other defense companies, which saw the writing on the wall much later.

From 1990 to 1992, General Dynamics sold businesses in aerospace, land systems, and electronics. By 1992 it had reduced the company to three core businesses and $3.5 billion in revenues, a 70 percent reduction in three years. Amazingly, at the same time, through operating improvements the company increased profitability from a minus 8 percent in 1990 to plus 8 percent in 1992.

At that point, the company began reinvesting in the business, making selective acquisitions to bolster its profitable submarine core and build a new, related core in electronics and information systems for defense programs. From 1992 through 2005, the company's revenues grew from $3.5 billion to $21.2 billion. General Dynamics was the best-performing defense company in the United States during this period.

The story of General Dynamics illustrates how dramatic change in the profit pool can trigger the need to redefine a company. It also demonstrates the power of seeing and acting on insights preemptively, before the competition. Certainly, in some cases the shift in a profit pool leaves an opportunity for some competitors to stay behind and serve the old market for a while; examples include niche sellers of black-and-white film, or video rental businesses. In general, however, when the profit pool shifts in a major way, you are better off figuring out how you also need to shift.

Situation 2: Direct Threat to the Core Model

A serious direct threat from a competitor with a new and superior business model was the most frequent and primary trigger for a company to redefine the core. The warning signs appear first in market share losses at the fringes of your business, a few steps away from core customers. Then the new competitor starts to creep closer toward your profitable core. At that point, it's often too late to react successfully.

The most-difficult-to-counter threat is a new competitor with a new business model that has inherently superior economics, especially cost levels. It can be difficult to spot such a threat, because it requires looking at your business in a new light and accurately assessing competitors' costs, which are not always that easy to establish with a high level of certainty. My team analyzed twenty-four situations of major market share loss by companies that had clear industry leadership, even temporary dominance, followed by significant decline. We found that most of these companies were slow to react to a mortal threat to the heart of their business. The list of examples is long: CBS's reaction to CNN; General Motors' reaction to Toyota; Compaq's reaction to Dell; Kmart's reaction to Wal-Mart; Sainsbury's reaction to Tesco; Xerox's reaction to Canon, and so on. The challenge of embracing an alternative business model, and possibly even cannibalizing yourself in the process, requires a step toward redefining a traditional core that few companies have taken successfully.

Similarly, in five of the case studies in this book, the impetus for redefining the core came from specific, direct assaults by a competitor or the emergence of a superior competitive model. PSA Corporation is one example.

PSA Corporation: No Shelter from Cost and Price Umbrellas. For years, the government-owned PSA Corporation (PSA) had earned extraordinary returns—net profit margins consistently between 35 and 40 percent—through its dominance of the container traffic through the Straits of Malacca, one of the most heavily frequented waterways in the world. Yet in 2000, PSA's high prices and high costs, combined with a downturn in the global container shipping industry, created a crisis in the core. Competitors in other ports were taking advantage of PSA's high prices to lure customers away.

A case in point was the Port of Tanjung Pelepas in Malaysia, which boasted costs and prices more than 30 percent lower than PSA's. In 2000, PSA's two largest customers—Maersk Sealand (the world leader in container shipping) and Evergreen (a gigantic Taiwanese company)—announced that they were moving their business to another port. As a result, business at PSA dropped 9 percent.

PSA reacted with intensity to renew its core. It changed top management and cut costs dramatically. To prevent further customer defections, PSA went all out, offering customers special deals and allowing them to invest in and control their own berthing facilities, in return for a long-term commitment to stay in Singapore—a change many of its largest customers, including Maersk, had requested for years. PSA also continued to invest aggressively in locations beyond Singapore (it now has investments in twenty-five ports in fourteen countries around the world). Today, PSA is back on track, but it had to dramatically change its strategy and tear apart the cost and price umbrella it had built up over the years.

Cost and price umbrellas encourage new competitors to go after your core, making it look highly profitable, even easy pickings. High costs and prices allow weaker competitors to thrive and strengthen. They're especially dangerous for companies when a rival with a new model and superior cost structure enters the picture.

A once-strong core business can encounter direct challenges for several reasons. Most common is an inherently lower-cost economic structure, as in the case of PSA and as we are seeing with the emerging stream of low-cost competitors in the airline business. Google's rapid shift from attacker to strong leader in Internet search derived from the company's superior search engine and algorithms, which spawned a much better economic model for the customers (better searches faster) and for Google (higher advertising revenue and traffic). A third type of challenge is the emergence of new capabilities, such as the development of biotechnology in the pharmaceutical industry.

Situation 3: Stall-Out of the Growth Formula

To borrow the words of poet T. S. Eliot, the need to redefine may come "not with a bang but a whimper." The whimper in this case is the sound of a once-valuable source of competitive differentiation eroding. It might be a business in which the competitors have caught up, eroding your lead. Or it might be a business in which a once-decisive low-cost business model has been mimicked or has gradually lost effectiveness, forcing the industry to look for new ways to differentiate. No competitive formula lasts forever, and when it does, financial stagnation is often not far behind. Fewer than one in five companies that stalls out for five years or more (defined as revenue and profit growth declining to near zero or less) can come close to its prior growth and profitability in the next five years.

There are three primary ways that a growth formula can run out of gas. The first way is through success. The formula has run its course, as at the end of the game of Pac-Man, when the little man on the screen has finally eaten all the coins in the game. There are no more. Vodafone, for instance, had an astonishing fifteen-year growth trajectory based on preemptively acquiring other cellular phone companies, in one country after another, faster and more effectively than competitors. But eventually you run out of countries, everyone has a cell phone, and you need to shift focus, perhaps to selling more sophisticated services over the phone, to developing the retail channel, to integrating phone and broadband services to the home, or to something else. The alternative is a stall-out.

In a second way a growth formula exhausts itself, plenty of new territory exists to be conquered but the cost-benefit equation of winning these new battles begins to change unfavorably. Either competitors are tougher in successive territories, or your potential customers value your offering less than the first adopters.

Perhaps an emerging example of this is Wal-Mart. Despite its amazing power and unquestioned success, the company's ability to extend its formula into other markets, from Germany and South Korea (it withdrew from both countries last year after large multiyear investments) to the United Kingdom (through its ASDA chain, which was experiencing difficulties in 2006), has proven problematic. The differentiations underlying the company's U.S. success formula have proven to have limits in other markets. How Wal-Mart will change its growth equation, adapting its model, will be one of the major stories to follow over the next few years.

The third, and most difficult, way that a growth formula runs down is for its natural advantage to erode, jeopardizing territory the company has conquered and reducing the odds of winning in new areas.

Before executives prepare to make a fundamental change, they must diagnose whether a stall-out is temporary. Among our case studies, the companies whose growth formulas stalled over the long haul include Brunswick in marine motors and boats, De Beers in diamonds, and Autodesk in computer-aided design—all stories told at length in this book. Figure 2-2 summarizes these situations.

FIGURE 2-2

Situations that often require strategic redefinition

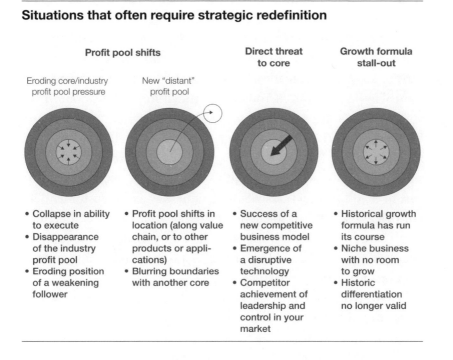

Profit pool shifts		Direct threat to core	Growth formula stall-out
Eroding core/industry profit pool pressure	New "distant" profit pool		
• Collapse in ability to execute	• Profit pool shifts in location (along value chain, or to other products or applications)	• Success of a new competitive business model	• Historical growth formula has run its course
• Disappearance of the industry profit pool	• Blurring boundaries with another core	• Emergence of a disruptive technology	• Niche business with no room to grow
• Eroding position of a weakening follower		• Competitor achievement of leadership and control in your market	• Historic differentiation no longer valid

The State of the Core Diagnostic

Managers are surrounded by an increasingly thick cocoon of data on their business, and yet little of it matters very much. Today's corporate information systems have an impressive ability to collect, slice, and dice financial data around the world by country, product, or customer. These systems are getting better at assigning costs where they belong, creating ever more precise measures. But of what? More than ever before, I'm hearing executives say that they feel as if they receive more data, but less information about what really matters in making the most important decisions.

Numbers are the lingua franca of business. Yet by creating an impressive Tower of Babel of internal financial metrics, is it possible that we are overlooking the more fundamental need for information about the hidden strategic balance sheet? Furthermore, as the world speeds up, do these positional indicators become less telling even while they are becoming so much better?

It is as if managers are driving a fast car with state-of-the-art rearview mirrors and position-finding technology. Yet even as the car's positional information improves, the terrain ahead becomes more winding and treacherous. As a result, information about where you were in the past, or even where you are right this minute, becomes less critical to decisions regarding the future. This is a tough dynamic. In our Growth Survey, managers reported that the shelf lives of strategies are rapidly decreasing (81 percent say it is true in their business). They felt the same way about customer data (74 percent say it is obsolete much sooner) and about competitive data (80 percent). One implication is that you need to pay more attention to both the hidden asset side and the liability side of what amounts to a strategic balance sheet.

There is no single business litmus test that turns pink where there is a hidden liability and shows blue if there is not. The unseen dynamics in an industry are too complex for that. Yet it is essential for executives to gain a clear understanding of the company's current competitiveness and its future market dynamics. It's amazing to me how many internal executive surveys I have seen—of the top, say, one hundred managers of a company—in which only about 20 to 30 percent believe that they understand their customers well, understand their competitors well, or agree on what will happen in the future. Analyses of the way senior executives spend their time show consistently that they devote a small percentage of time to looking at dynamics outside the company, spending most of their time on internal issues.

These studies show that senior managers spend less than 3 percent of their time developing a long-term view of the future of their industry. They spend about 40 percent on issues outside their four walls (customers, competitors, etc.). Of that time, about 30 percent (or 12 percent of their total time) is focused on issues having implications more than two years out; and of that time, about 20 percent is spent with their management team figuring out where the business is heading in the future.[4] All the evidence that we have suggests that, if anything, executives' line of sight into the future has shortened as the speed of business has increased and as management turnover has escalated.

Figure 2-3 contains a five-part state of the core diagnostic. I have seen these questions used many times to assess the state of the key source of competitive differentiation in the core business, whether it is in danger of eroding, and, if so, why. Each of these questions gets at something different from the typical operating and financial metrics that populate management reports. Yet these five questions are among the most central of all, and some of the most difficult ones to see accurately because we are so close to them. It is like appraising a key personal relationship or judging your own health. These areas that are closest to us may be the ones where new, objective data can be the most revelatory. I have found this equally true in studying business situations.

The first set of questions involves the definition and state of the core customer. Often, it's difficult to determine which customers are at the very core of the business and why—the most profitable, the

FIGURE 2-3

State of the core diagnostic

Questions	Key indicators
1. What is the state of the core customer?	• Profitability • Market capture • Retention rate • Net Promoter Score • Share of wallet
2. What is the state of the core differentiation?	• Definition and metrics of differentiation • Relative cost position • Importance: increasing or decreasing
3. What is the state of the industry profit pool?	• Size, growth, and stability • Capture • Boundaries • Shifts and projection • Quality—cost and price umbrellas
4. What is the state of the core capabilities?	• Inventory key capabilities • Relative importance • Gaps versus competitors • Gaps versus future core needs
5. What is the state of the organization— is it ready to execute and adapt to change?	• Loyalty and undesired attrition • Capacity and stress points • Alignment and agreement with objectives • Energy and motivation to change • Ability to implement growth

most loyal, the most valuable. But defining your core customer is the essential first step of creating your strategy.

The second question probes the key sources of competitive differentiation, querying whether they are strengthening (or eroding) and defining their root cause. Third, it is critical to explore the industry profit pool—not only the market's size and growth. Where can profits be earned? Who earns them? Why? How will this change?

Capabilities, the building blocks of business, are the topic of the fourth question. Chapter 5 looks closely at this issue of defining and assessing your current core capabilities and needs for the future. Capabilities are almost always the building blocks of strategic redefinition.

The fifth question is about the softer, but no less important, side of the equation: the state of the organization and its readiness for change.

Clearly, any of these areas could be expanded into an almost infinite list of increasingly detailed questions. But if you can answer these questions clearly and convincingly, you have a good start in contemplating whether and how to change.

Companies that are concerned that their differentiation is eroding or that their core model might need to be renewed should begin with this diagnostic exercise. It helps you establish the base case, the state of the core, and the most likely future trajectory in the absence of a change in strategy. The elements of this diagnostic can point the way toward the path to renewal, as revealed in the case of Avis Rent A Car.

Avis: Hitting Unseen Bumps in the Road

The Avis car rental company is a powerful illustration of how a thorough examination of the state of the core can identify or confirm a series of threats that demand action. Avis discovered that it faced the perfect storm, with problems brewing on all three dimensions. First, industry profit pools were shrinking, making the entire business more price sensitive and foreshadowing a decade of continued consolidation of local players, regional franchisees, and even some majors (and that is what happened). Second, a new competitive model (embodied in Enterprise Rent-A-Car's model to serve the replacement market) had created the most profitable rental car company in the world, with potential ripple effects into other segments at the cores of Avis and Hertz. Third, differentiation among car rental companies had narrowed in general, creating a strong need to find new ways of competing.

To the average outsider, Avis looks like a company that has stuck to its formula over the past decade; it's still using a red logo, still renting cars, still in airports, still "trying harder" in its advertising.

Yet when you look under the hood, you see an operational transformation followed by a profound strategic repositioning.

In 1994, the business founded by Warren Avis forty-eight years earlier was sputtering and threatening to coast to the side of the road and stop dead. The company had experienced a 70 percent profit decline, to $30 million, and was about to lose money. Avis was at the bottom in the J.D. Power survey of service levels, and it was losing market share in its core car rental market (the top one hundred airports in the United States).

There was considerable discussion and difference of opinion among the management team about the cause of the problem. Some of them felt that the cyclical nature of industry pricing had caught them off-guard. Wait and it will turn around, they counseled. Others thought that certain cost areas, especially the corporate headquarters, and real estate costs were the key to the equation. Still others wanted to pursue the profitable replacement segment of the market that Enterprise had created and led.

But the answer didn't lie in any of these areas. Instead, it came through revelations regarding three liabilities that had been growing under the surface and whose consequences were now being seen everywhere. Avis detected these liabilities during an extensive self-evaluation done with the agreement of the full management team, a conversation where no issues were left untouched. Each liability was in an area that company systems did not track (but do now): competitive cost position (Avis proved to be high cost even against Hertz); retention and repeat rental behaviors of the most valuable frequent-renter segment (not well targeted and exhibiting a high and poorly recognized churn rate); and industry profit pool dynamics (which would soon drive consolidation among competitors at airports).

These insights were not obtained by reflection and discussion alone but by an effort built around five key diagnostics of the health of the Avis core business. The first diagnostic was a thorough X-ray of competitor economics that went well beyond what you can read in competitors' annual reports. It essentially involved reverse engineering the competitors' cost positions and profit sources. The result was a series of new insights about Avis's unacceptable cost position.

The second diagnosis involved looking at long-term price and cost trajectories per rental unit over several decades, trying to separate what was cyclical and what was secular. The results showed that the rental car business exhibited a very regular price and cost decline of around 1 percent per year, with different cycles within that curve. The implication was the need to plan for increasingly tight cost management and not to assume that price would be the savior.

The third diagnostic was an analysis of the long-term industry profit pool, an assessment that led management to develop a unified point of view on the long-term future of the industry. Well before consolidation actually happened, the group concluded that it was inevitable.

The fourth diagnostic looked closely at the customer base and especially the important frequent-renter group; it led Avis to make a number of enhancements to its loyalty program (its President's Club) and to improve tracking in its database.

The final element was culture. Internal discussions and interviews revealed that the repeated buying and selling of the company had caused high frustration among the staff, but also that they had a strong desire to make major changes.

All five of the key areas of the state of the core diagnostic were relevant for Avis, it turned out, and each had action implications. Three in particular (competitive cost, profit pool compression, and the need to shore up the frequent-renter business) led to immediate actions on the part of CEO Joe Vittoria, Chief Operating Officer (now president and COO) Bob Salerno, and their team. This state of the core diagnostic revealed hidden liabilities that simply had to be addressed—and to the credit of the management team, it addressed them.

For instance, analysis of competition showed that Avis had a high-cost position even when compared with gold-plated and corporately owned leader Hertz, which had about 30 percent market share compared with about 20 percent for Avis. Avis was an ESOP company (an employee-owned company) whose internal stock price had declined in the previous two years from $17 to $9 and was continuing to slide. The company was headquartered on Long Island in a gigantic, decaying structure contaminated with asbestos, a symbol of the difficulty of making change.

Furthermore, before the ESOP, Avis had been bought and sold repeatedly by a string of corporations that seemed to compete with each other for who could invest the least. Bob Salerno said, "When we went from Norton Simon to Esmark to Beatrice, these companies were not buying Avis, they were buying the parent and did not care about the rental car business, and so it was sold over and over and squeezed for cash at every turn."[5] The effect of this constant buying and selling on the mind-set of the organization could be seen as another form of psychological, internal liability below the surface. Almost fittingly, Avis proudly continued to base its advertising on its once famous (now changed) slogan: "We're number two, but we try harder."[6]

Today, Avis has a different engine under the hood. The company has outgrown the industry, reaching $4 billion in revenues and $434 million in operating profit, the best of any airport-focused competitor in the world. In 2003 the J.D. Power survey rated Avis number 1 in service. A company whose accounting department did not have any computers in 1994 is now the number 1 online-rental-car site by volume, ahead of traditional competitors like Hertz and also ahead of new travel sites like Orbitz. Avis acquired the troubled Budget Rent-a-Car to implement a dual brand strategy at airports, but combined backroom facilities to create industry-leading scale. What is now called the Avis Budget Group has risen to 34 percent total share of rentals at airports.

If you calculate what one share of Avis, bought in the dark days of the ESOP in 1994, would return if held through today, you discover that the financial gain would be about 20 times return on investment. Furthermore, Avis now has the best on-airport economic platform in the industry in both relative competitive cost position and scale. Finally, Avis has retained the important cultural mantra "We try harder." As Bob Salerno says, "'We try harder' is the ethos of the company and is built into its fabric in lots of detailed ways. It is very powerful and surprisingly important to the employees. The research done by every advertising firm for the past decade has said not to touch that part of it. It has real meaning to people at the core. One reason the ESOP was powerful for a while was actually because of that belief, that bond. But we have definitely stopped saying we are number 2."[7] That's because it is no longer true.

The questions posed in the state of the core diagnostic are central to running a business to its full potential over the short, the medium, and the longer term.

Strengthening the Platform Before Redefining

Making a fundamental change in your core business robs scarce resources—management time, cash, people, organizational attention—from other activities. The senior executives interviewed for this book often indicated that they underestimated the complexity, the physical exhaustion, and the amount of resources involved in successful change. As you go through this book, it's a good idea to visualize the extra effort required to conceive and execute a change program at the same time that you are running a business, often under the scrutiny of investors who do not understand the nature of your efforts to grow the company in the long term.

About two-thirds of the cases we looked at—across the full range of starting points from crisis to stall-out to sustainable—included some form of restructuring or operational performance improvement phase. Clearly, as its story indicates, Avis did this for years. The transformation of PerkinElmer to Applera, discussed in chapter 3, involved reducing costs in the historic core by nearly 20 percent. The amazing resurrection of Samsung involved a restructuring office, set up at the start of the project, that spearheaded radical change to strengthen and focus the platform (through dives-titures, staff reductions, and process quality programs). Some com-panies have even found that they needed to reduce their activities before moving forward—in a sense, shrinking to grow. This was a paradox that we saw repeatedly.

This book, and the entire topic of redefinition, contains in every chapter and example a single theme that runs throughout, like the voices of a fugue in music—interacting in new ways, morphing, but never going away. That is the theme of leadership and of the eco-nomics of leadership. This does not mean that our methods require that you eventually become the market leader by size in your indus-try; that would be wrong and seldom a worthwhile concept. It does mean that you need to find an area of unique strength to build on—a core: a set of customer situations, channels, locations, or products where you are as good as anyone and where you have something to leverage competitively.

Our entire discussion of hidden assets can be viewed as a set of lenses through which you look at current, or potential, leadership economics—in a customer, in a business, in a product line, or in a capability. That said, it is important to pause and reflect on some of the dimensions of leadership economics: where it comes from, what it can mean, why it is important. Let's look at three dimensions: the power of leadership, the dilemma of being a distant follower, and the observation that often the best first step to redefinition might actu-ally be to shrink to a stable core before you launch a new strategy.

The Power of Leadership Economics

Hidden assets are ultimately about the search for small pockets of superiority, differentiation, leadership, and the economics that are attendant on leadership. This is true for new platforms (chapter 3) and for the search for hidden customer segments (chapter 4). It even applies in some ways to capabilities. We return to the concept of hidden assets after a brief but essential digression on the value of leadership economics. For, if you peel away the layers in most of my case examples to get to the very center of the story, you usually find a kernel of underexploited market power and influence in the form of a customer position or a product market position (platform) or a capability.

Consider the following facts that emerge from our analysis of the economics of leadership in a well-defined competitive arena.

- The typical industry has more than six competitors. The top two competitors usually capture more than 75 percent of the profit pool, and the company with the greatest market power usually captures about 70 percent of total profits and 75 percent of profits above the cost of capital (figure 2-4).

- Followers are the shock absorbers of the economic system, exhibiting much larger fluctuations and signs of weakness during downturns. When we analyzed twenty-two pairs of clear global leaders and followers (Nike versus Reebok; Southwest Airlines versus Delta; Intel versus AMD; Medtronic versus St. Jude Medical; Bridgestone versus Continental, and so on), we found that the average variance in profit margin was three times as great for followers as leaders. This discrepancy should give strong leaders an inherent advantage in making gains during downturns, because their relative economics are magnified profoundly compared with those of struggling followers.

- Capital markets value leaders at a premium relative to followers in the same industry. In the same twenty-two paired comparisons, the ratio of market value to book value was used as a measure of premiums that the market placed on leaders. We found that leaders had nearly twice the market-to-book ratio of followers. This gives leaders an inherent advantage in raising money, in controlling their costs of debt service, in making acquisitions, and in rewarding employees.

- Leaders in the paired comparisons also sustained a 33 percent higher reinvestment rate than followers, while maintaining higher margins and lower costs—a formidable combination.

- Leaders have a greater success rate at driving their core business into areas within two steps of their core. Even with relatively close-in growth moves, clear followers have a success rate of only about 17 percent. Companies at parity enjoy success rates as high as the overall average of 27 percent, and clear leaders have success rates of more than 40 percent. Again, if properly managed, this difference can be a huge advantage when it comes to growth and value creation over time. Strong leaders have much more loyal customers, as shown by their Net Promoter Scores.[8] Net Promoter Scores are an index developed by my colleague Fred Reichheld to measure customer loyalty through customers' willingness to recommend a product to others. For instance, for Southwest Airlines the score is 51 percent, compared with only 11 percent for Delta. Some companies, such as Harley-Davidson, have scores of 80 percent—off the chart. It's very hard for a follower to compete with traditional means in the current market definition.

FIGURE 2-4

Leaders capture the profit pool

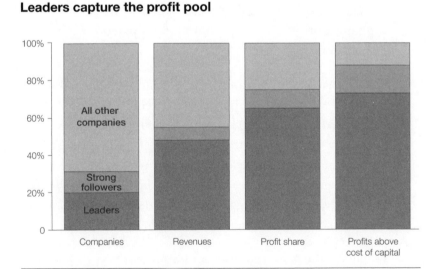

The Curse of the Distant Follower

Given the emphasis on the power of leadership—even in a single segment, product, or situation—what can distant followers do? Is there hope in jumping to a new lily pad? The answer isn't rapid acting magic but rather a hard slog to achieve an island of leadership economics, a core to build on. We examined 402 followers (clear number 3 or lower) in fifty-one sectors in Japan, and 399 followers in the United States in the same fifty-one sectors. We studied the trajectories of these 801 companies from 1990 through 2001 to understand how many followers actually move into the leader's circle. The answer is that only about 10 percent do, in either country. Moreover, more than 30 percent of followers slipped back further in the pack in both countries.

The followers that did gain and moved up to become one of the top two companies in their market did so almost always for one of three reasons. The first reason was the development of an innovative product that the leader did not match. This action allowed about 4 percent of the followers at the start of the decade to leap into the leadership group. Examples include Sony in video games with the PlayStation, Asahi Beer with its development of dry beer in 1987, and Nokia with its unique approach to phone design and its seizing of the high ground with GSM handsets.

The second way that followers reversed their position was by harnessing a unique strength in a narrow market segment as a platform for rebuilding their growth strategy in a unique way. One example is Enterprise Rent-A-Car's success in becoming the world's largest car rental company based on leadership in the replacement and body shop segments. Finally, a number of former followers seized control over the industry profit pool with a low-cost model that afforded them true market power and influence despite their smaller size. Examples are Amazon.com in books and Southwest Airlines.

Despite these positive examples, the record of distant followers moving up, or transforming themselves successfully, is dismal. The best hope, as the lessons of this section emphasize, appears to be finding an area of differential competitive advantage deep within the company, an island of leadership economics, and reforming the strategy from there. Very often, companies do not know their true economics by product, customer, or situation. This means that followers often have pockets of leadership that they do not fully recognize.

The alternative to reforming around a sustainable core is to wait for a bolt of product innovation lightning or to jump far from the core into unknown territory in search of a hot market. However, in general (and I will repeat this often), the odds of success for that approach are equivalent to playing the lottery and calling it your transformation strategy. And playing the lottery is not usually what investors or employees want from their leadership teams.

Royal Vopak: Shrinking to Grow

When you uncover an underutilized source of leadership economics, sometimes the best response is to "double down" on your investment in that area. A bold version of this, followed by all too few companies in need of a stronger platform, is the concept of actually shrinking to grow. Consider the example below of Vopak.

If you are not in the oil or chemicals business, you have probably not heard of Royal Vopak. This company is the world leader in independent tank storage of bulk oil and chemicals in seventy-five port locations, from Rotterdam to Houston to Singapore. In the past few years, Vopak has been one of the best-performing stocks in the Netherlands. But it has not always been that way. Vopak traces its roots back to a time when the Netherlands was the most powerful and wealthiest country in the world, based on its role as a center for shipping and trade with the Far East. The origins of Vopak lie in a company called Pakhuismeesteren, which was founded in 1616 by a group of porters at the docks of Rotterdam for the purpose of loading and unloading ship cargoes.

By 2001, Vopak was a €5.6 billion business, with positions in shipping (it owned tankers), chemical distribution, and storage facilities at ports. The storage facility business was the most profitable and had the strongest position. When Vopak's profits and stock price came under severe pressure, plummeting from €25 per share in July 1999 to €12 in July 2002, the company took decisive action. It spun off all its businesses except for the storage business, reducing the size of the company to €750 million. But it did not stop there. Even within the portfolio of storage locations, the company sold additional business, further reducing its size.

What was the result? Amazingly, the market value of the company increased beyond its original value, as the stock price rebounded to €30 in May 2006. Furthermore, the stronger, well-funded business began to grow again—both organically and through acquisitions and new port locations. During the first half of 2006, Vopak grew revenues organically by 17 percent, and earnings by 28 percent, in an inherently low-growth industry. CEO John Paul Broeders says, "Without shrinking first, we would never have created the resources, the management focus, and a stable platform to begin to grow again as we have."[9] Shrinking to grow may be starting to gain popularity as a realistic gambit to renew a flagging core. Indeed, three of the twenty-five case studies used this tactic with great success: PerkinElmer, Samsung, and GUS.

Shrink to grow strategies are not an end in themselves, but they are a useful tactic to pave the way for redefinition. We find that these moves have a very high success rate—about two out of three—when it comes to increasing a company's value and liberating one of the cores (with additional resources) to strengthen and grow. This is consistent with the findings described in *Profit from the Core,* my first book on strategic focus, and has been further validated by academic research.

I close with the brief example of Samsung Electronics to illustrate the key points of this section.

Samsung: Stabilizing the Platform to Redefine

For much of the 1990s, few investors wanted to own Korean conglomerate Samsung. It was notorious for low-quality products, and its name didn't appear on anyone's list of leading brands. Its financials seemed to be in a free fall: in one year its market value declined 60 percent, its profits 95 percent. Even Samsung Electronics, the jewel in the company's crown, was running into problems. Although it held the top position worldwide in memory chips, for instance, it was a distant number 5 in the fast-growing mobile-phone industry. By 1998 the company's situation was so bad that Chairman Kun-Hee Lee told his employees, "We are facing the worst crisis ever . . . where survival itself is uncertain. I am ready to give up my money, honor, and life to overcome the crisis."[10]

Fortunately, Lee didn't have to give up any of these things; instead, he guided the company to a dramatic recovery. Samsung's market value increased from $2 billion in 1996 to $78 billion in 2005. Its operating-profit margins rose from 4 percent to 21 percent. The company's name was no longer a liability; indeed, it was now rated among the world's twenty most valuable brands. In consumer electronics Samsung has become one of the most feared competitors anywhere. At this writing it occupies a top slot not only in memory chips and mobile phones but also in high-end television sets and flat-screen monitors.

Samsung is an example of a company that let its situation approach the brink and then systematically attacked its problems using a corporate restructuring office that it still maintains. It moved successfully from restructuring to massive cost reduction to a complete strategic redirection and organizational overhaul. Consider the initiatives undertaken by the company. They hold specific lessons for others, and they are an appropriate way to close this chapter on capabilities.

Focus and shrink to grow. Samsung hit the wall financially while participating in an increasingly challenging global business against competitors that were constantly investing in technology. Samsung had to liberate resources to focus on stabilizing its core. It shut down thirty-four businesses throughout the company (such as small home appliances), sold another forty-two low-value-added businesses, and shut down more than two hundred fifty major internal investment projects. The company focused the bulk of its efforts on Samsung Electronics, which contained its semiconductor business and its consumer electronics, such as televisions.

Stabilize the cost base. A benign home market had allowed the chaebol structure (Korean family-owned conglomerates) to flourish, with Samsung Electronics being run as a cash cow to fund a range of other businesses that were not strong enough to fund themselves. In a world of increasingly difficult global competition, this became an impossible burden for Samsung. The same was true of its layers of long-tenured employees, a structure that was attacked intensely by the Samsung restructuring office, driving Samsung Electronics from 84,000 employees in 1996 to 42,000 by 1999. With cost tightening also came asset tightening in the supply chain, the next focus of the team. It quickly drove out underperforming product lines and reduced inventory by 8 billion Korean won (₩) from 1997 to 1999.

Strengthen operating capabilities and the platform. Perhaps the most long-lasting change, and in some ways the most surprising, was Samsung's ability to identify and infuse best practices for product quality and cycle-time reduction into its core semiconductor business. This business was an under-leveraged asset by virtue of its position as one of the top three global suppliers in most forms of chips, from DRAM (memory) to LSI (microprocessors systems on chips).

The company flew in planeloads of technical consultants from all over the world, especially Japan, during this period, trying to become the world's best-practice producer at each stage of semiconductor manufacturing. In the process, Samsung went from average to the best at cycle time for building a new semiconductor fabrication facility, as well as the fastest to get to high yields (a measure of efficiency) on new products from those plants. Samsung had liberated the potential of its leading, but previously inefficient, semiconductor business to fuel its next investment, high-end consumer electronic products. It was one of the few companies to possess all the technologies in this segment, and the only one to be as strong and low cost in as many product lines.

Shortly afterward, Samsung went from a laggard in the filing of scientific patents to one of the world leaders (from three hundred annual patent filings in the early 1990s to fourteen hundred in the late 1990s).

Add new capabilities to redefine the growth model. With this platform, Samsung dialed up its investment in selected areas of consumer electronics products, where it possessed core technology and was able to hire top design talent. Now it is a leader in a series of consumer markets such as monitors, VCRs, flat-panel displays, and cellular phones. Seemingly overnight, Samsung has moved from nowhere to the top 20 most valued consumer brands in the world.

Today, Samsung's restructuring office continues its mission of driving major, companywide programs and of searching outside Korea for best practices to adopt and to benchmark against. Few other major companies have such an aggressive, empowered internal organization. It is interesting that more than twenty business unit heads have come through the restructuring office and the education it provides.

Managing the Strategic Balance Sheet

This book argues three simple points. First, more companies than ever before will discover that their once-successful growth formula is approaching natural limits and will need to examine the prospect of making fundamental changes (some for the first time) in their core. Second, the warning signs of change are revealed less in typical financials and operating ratios and more in structural indicators and liabilities lurking below the surface (measurable in our state of the core diagnostic). Third, the most successful cases of transformation are modular or gradual in nature, target leadership economics in the new core (versus, for example, hot markets), seek a repeatable formula for growth, and build on hidden assets.

Redefining the core is not always possible, and it may not be the right thing to do in some cases. Some companies will find no viable solution to the collapse of their profit pool, the attack of a disruptive technology, or the finality with which their past growth formula suddenly runs out of runway. The answer for these companies is to go through the process of looking at their hidden assets, trying to find a sensible solution to the problem by following the ideas in this book to improve the odds that such a solution will be found—if it exists. But not all businesses can be redefined, and not all have a path to the future that does not destroy value. In those cases, the answer may be to combine with a competitor that has a brighter future, to combine with a company that has what you are missing, or to slowly liquidate and generate cash to return to the shareholders.

The least attractive courses—the ones that the statistical record shows destroy most value—are the bold moves of desperation: leaping to a hot market, piling all your chips on a risky new technology, or going for a big-bang move with your remaining resources. The record of success here is not much better than a pure lottery. This book is about understanding the odds and illustrating a proven method to finding a path to renewal, where it exists. This book does not guarantee that such redefinition is always the answer or can always be done with attractive economics. The worst tragedy of all is to take the destructive path or to give up, when a clear, value-creating alternative exists through a new strategy built upon hidden assets. I hope that this book can help even a few companies to avoid this fate.

We now turn to the hidden assets that can reignite your growth and ways you can make the most of them to renew your core business.

3

Undervalued Business Platforms

At the heart of this book, and of our findings overall, is the idea that the past phases of a company's growth inevitably collect and foster a range of hidden assets that very often prove to be central to the strategy of the future. This does not mean that they solve the problem or that looking outside your company is unnecessary. On the contrary, strategic renewal almost always requires acquiring some new capability. The insight is that many components of renewal already existed within a given company but had not been fully valued for their future role in generating growth. That is why we refer to them as *hidden assets*. It's not that companies ignore their existence, rather that they discount their utility and true long-term value by orders of magnitude.

We have defined three main categories of hidden assets that are critical in the case studies we examined. The first category, described in this chapter, consists of assets that could become the epicenter of a new wave of growth, either as an entirely new business or as a way to redefine the center of gravity of the old core business. These can be a set of adjacency moves that combine to create the fulcrum for a new strategy, an underused support function, or an undervalued business product or family.

The case of PerkinElmer below illustrates how a hidden business platform—in this case, a set of products—can suddenly provide the key to redefining the core of the company and renewing its growth.

PerkinElmer: Changing the DNA

As a child, Dick Perkin was fascinated by astronomy. At age thirteen he began grinding and polishing his own telescope lenses in his parents' basement. At age thirty-one he and a partner, Charles Elmer, founded a company in Manhattan to fabricate precision optical components. The year was 1937.

By the time World War II broke out, the young company's reputation for precision optics had spread, and it became the main U.S. source for tank periscopes and aerial reconnaissance. When the war ended, PerkinElmer, as it was called, entered the emerging world of optical electronics for analytic instruments such as spectrophotometers and gas chromatographs, where it quickly became the market leader. The company was also a leader in the manufacture of large telescopes. In 1957 the U.S. government called on PerkinElmer to track the path of Sputnik I, the Russian satellite whose launch had shocked the nation. Later, the company manufactured the Hubble Space Telescope for the National Aeronautics and Space Administration.[1]

In the early 1990s, almost by happenstance, PerkinElmer branched out in another direction through a strategic alliance with Cetus Corp. to develop products for amplifying DNA. In the process PerkinElmer obtained the rights to cutting-edge procedures known as polymerase chain reaction (PCR) technology. In what was considered within the company to be a highly contentious move, it also acquired Applied Biosystems (AB), a small Silicon Valley life-sciences equipment company.

But nothing seemed to restore the earlier magic. By 1993 PerkinElmer's core markets were stagnant. The company was under attack by lower-cost competitors. Revenues were stuck at $1.2 billion, exactly what they had been ten years earlier, and the bottom line showed a loss of $83 million. Over the preceding decade, the company's market position had eroded and it had created no economic value for shareholders. The board wanted a CEO who would carve out a new path for the business. The man they found, Tony White, had enjoyed a successful twenty-six-year tenure with Baxter International and was looking for a new challenge to cap his career. There was only one problem: the company he took over in 1995 had no growth, low profits, and no plan to fix the situation. White remembers:

> When I came along the company was really struggling. My first instinct was that you had to completely change this company, invest heavily in its small life-sciences instrument line, fix the profitability problem of the original instrument business, and use the returns from that business to fund the new core. After some work I concluded that the transformation was risky but that it could be done. So I took the job. I had a good idea of what I wanted to do before I became CEO and refined the plan when I began. I wanted to do something significant and thought that the only way was to try to turn the company from a declining old-line lab-instrument business into the company that would be seen as having the most focused commitment to the new life-sciences industry.
>
> PerkinElmer, almost by accident, had obtained early access to and coownership of PCR technology. In 1993, they bought Applied Biosystems. It was acquired as just another line of instruments that would be integrated and add some new product numbers in their catalogs.
>
> I was struck by how misconceived it was to tear AB apart and distribute its parts across the functions in the organization. I thought, "Here is a company whose management does not see what they have." So one of the first steps I took was to begin to reassemble the parts of AB. I appointed a new president of the division, Mike Hunkapiller, and announced that I was going to reform

the core of the company over a three-year period around this unique platform with leadership in the key life-sciences detection technology.[2]

White made a point to communicate openly and often:

> In one of my first communications to employees I decided not to be demure, but to tell them that the management team and I had decided to do this, with the plan to exit the original core within three years. I met with everybody individually or in small groups throughout the company to communicate the different roles of the original core and the new core. To execute on this transformation, we had to create incentives for people in each business that were different and reflected their particular role. In the original PerkinElmer business we decided to take $75 million to $100 million out of the cost structure, and we set about doing that. We actually found more cost savings even than that. In the AB business, we set a target to go from $400 million to $1 billion in revenues in three years by initiating a program that led to the Model 3700 gene sequencer product line.

White then made another important move: he hired maverick scientist Craig Venter to build a team that could use AB's gene-sequencing machines to sequence the complete human genome. If the team was successful it would be the first group in the world to achieve this amazing milestone, essentially unlocking the key to human life.

The company set up a subsidiary, Celera, with the goal of first sequencing the genome and later parlaying that into a data and diagnostic business. To fund this venture, White raised $1 billion in a secondary public offering. He also exited the company's original core of instrument manufacture, almost exactly on his original three-year timetable. The buyer, EG&G, based in Wellesley, Mass., paid $425 million for the instrument business—and promptly changed its corporate name to PerkinElmer. White, meanwhile, established a company named Applera, which would act as a holding company for both Applied Biosystems (which specialized in sequencing equipment and supplies) and Celera Genomics. To create a separate currency for fund-raising and valuation, Celera also issued a separate stock series, now a tracking stock. Says White:

> My grandfather said, "Never bet the company," but there are times when you sort of have to. This was one of them. I had strong confidence that we could sequence the human genome. I was delighted when the government decided to make it a race and challenge us, wanting not to be eclipsed by a private company. Unlike the original instrument business, the people in AB were younger, Silicon Valley types who were not risk averse and [who were] more concerned about flexibility and the social mission and less about job security. The underlying theme had to be, "We are going to change the world." You can tell your grandchildren that you helped on the route to curing cancer or Alzheimer's.

In one of the most dramatic business stories of the past decade, Celera won the race to become the first group to sequence the human genome. It beat the government-funded Human Genome Project, which included Dr. James Watson, the Nobel Prize–winning scientist who was codiscoverer of the double-helix structure of DNA.

It was a startling accomplishment. The genome is contained on the twenty-three pairs of chromosomes that are found in the nucleus of every cell. A strand of DNA is only 79 billionths of an inch wide, but it would run six feet in length if you could stretch it out. Each strand consists of a series of four chemical bases, like the letters that make up words in a book—but the genome has one billion words. It would take a human being more than 100 years of reading for eight hours each day to get to the end.[3] Since Celera's feat of sequencing the genome, the world has seen a wave of scientific and business applications in gene therapy, diagnostic testing, and methods to make drugs more precise in their actions on the human body. The feat has even led to a revolution in DNA-based identification and other forensic applications.

What was it that persuaded White to go against his grandfather's advice and bet the company? "I had strong confidence that we could sequence the human genome," he says. "I listened to our outside scientific advisers, such as our board member Arnie Levine, in addition to our own team. The decisive moment for me was in my car when Arnie Levine called me up after doing his own due diligence on the idea and said, 'We can do this.' I then said, 'I can't *not* do this now.' I felt I would never forgive myself—and my shareholders should not forgive me—if I did not go for it."[4]

The burst of excitement about the genome caused Celera's stock to spike at an astonishing $247 per share in March 2000, implying a valuation for this small company of $18 billion. More recently it has come down to earth. Still, shareholders who held on for the full transformation are happy: an investor holding PerkinElmer stock at the time White announced his strategy would have received about a 2,000 percent appreciation on the investment, not to mention owning part of the company that sequenced the human genome. Incidentally, even though Celera garnered the headlines, Applied Biosystems became the gold standard in the sequencing instrument business, with a strong leadership position in sequencers, as well as a robust platform for pursuing new opportunities in adjacent markets to leverage its $1.9 billion revenue and $275 million in net income.

PerkinElmer's story embodies many of our key findings in one remarkable example. First, the entire company, and not only its strategy, was reformed based on undervalued assets—gene sequencing equipment and supplies—that were buried deep in the catalogs along with other scientific instruments. Second, by selling the original equipment businesses, PerkinElmer first shrank to later grow, a move that is underused given its consistent record of liberating value. Third, the change process began with a wave of aggressive cost reduction and operating improvements to generate cash to fuel the new strategy and also to stabilize and strengthen the core instrument business for its new future.

Finally, the problems of PerkinElmer turned out to go deeper than the pure financials and market share numbers revealed. They went to the heart of the company's relative competitive cost position against foreign instrument companies, and a concerned customer base that was gradually eroding in the absence of sufficient innovation in new products.

PerkinElmer's People Challenge

The transformation of PerkinElmer highlights a number of practical problems of execution. How do you deal with a split organization whose parts have different missions? How do you deal with the natural dissonance created by a profound departure from the past?

Tony White and his team decided to be explicit from the start about the different roles of the old and the new organizations and the specific strategies and end points of each. They told managers in the legacy instrument business that they would evaluate success based on the smooth separation of life sciences, significant cost reduction and restructuring (such as plant closings and consolidations), and preparation of the business for sale or spin-off.

People who did not sign up for the mission received adequate notice, and some of them left. Those who stayed received a new set of incentives focusing on cash flow and cost targets, with the idea that PerkinElmer would find the best possible parent for the company. To make this real, White announced a clear time line from the start. "Everyone asks, 'What does this mean for me?'" White says. "This was especially important at the instrument company. I was religious about the time frame; otherwise, it would not have been believed. The three-year deadline was essential in retrospect." It's interesting that White's team did fulfill its promise of finding the best parent for the original core, selling the business to EG&G, which renamed itself PerkinElmer. It's not easy to split a company into two parts, each with an opposite role, a radically different strategic priority (grow versus strengthen operations), and a separate time frame. It required an unusual level of openness, sharply differing incentive packages, and a compelling logic about why this was the right path for both parts of the company. But it worked.

White commented extensively on this element:

> The most important part of the CEO job in situations like this is to build consensus. You cannot have loyalty without consensus. It is not the CEO showing up with new tablets and saying, "Read these." It is an iterative process that has to consider all points of view . . . As CEO you have lots of people who say they agree but really do not agree, so you have to constantly work at this dimension. We did breakfasts and lunches over and over at every level. You especially have to understand and take into consideration the very different needs of each segment in the company. The people in the instrument business had very different needs and aspirations than the Silicon Valley scientific types, who wanted to change the world with their genetic analysis products.

The unifying theme for both groups was the stock price, which increased through the efforts of each group and from which both benefited under the new incentive plan.

Companies with thousands of employees, complex networks of customers, legacies of previous strategies, and layers of complexity renew themselves when they are able to grow through a small number of patterns that are played repeatedly in industry after industry. These patterns blend several elements:

- Brilliant lateral thinking

- A clear and timely point of view on the future

- Awareness of the state of the core

- Hidden assets that were not central to the success formula of the past but now seem to hold the key to the future

New Centers of Gravity

Our study of the paths of the *Fortune* 500 companies suggests that 30 to 35 percent of the single-core companies that made significant changes in strategic direction did so by building on a hidden platform, an asset that was once peripheral but now assumes a position at center stage. In our twenty-five examples, about half redefined their strategies based on such an asset.

In a separate study, we analyzed a sample of 105 strategy cases undertaken by my company for clients pursuing the next wave of profitable growth and, often, strategic renewal. The managers who led the work reported that the types of hidden platforms described in this chapter were often central to the ultimate strategy. In 7 percent of the cases, the key platform asset was an underused product line; in 34 percent, a key element was a set of unexploited adjacency moves that created further strategic opportunities; and in 26 percent, a major capability or internal support function proved to have much more potential than had been realized.

We identified three primary types of platforms:

- Adjacencies (new geographies, new channels of distribution, and so on) that had been entered to expand the core business and now offer even more potential in their own right as the platform for a new strategy

- Support services and activities to the core (e.g., the customer service organization or a unique information system)

- Noncore businesses and orphan product groups

This chapter discusses each of these types of chronically undervalued assets. It also explains how to detect such assets and describes the business conditions that can act as pivots in helping rejuvenate a core business.

Not every company has such hidden platforms; clearly, many do not. Furthermore, some companies are so large that it would take several initiatives built on hidden assets to make a dent in overall strategy. However, in my experience, managers are not fully aware of all the assets that they have built up over the years and also do not look at them through a sufficiently rich, rigorous, or creative set of lenses. For those companies that possess such assets, it can make all the difference.

Platform 1: Adjacencies to the Core Business

In our prior research, reported in *Beyond the Core,* we found that most new growth in the average strong business comes from moves into so-called adjacencies surrounding the core: new geographies, new customer segments, new products or services, new steps in the value chain, or new channels. Extensive data analysis has shown that the odds of success for these individual moves are about 20 to 25 percent but that some companies develop a repeatable formula for growth that allows them to move much faster than their competitors, with much higher odds of success, for a period.

Adjacencies are the way most companies grow. Yet these unspectacular extensions to a business, flowing naturally from one to another, may combine in surprising ways to form a new platform for growth, or even the inspiration for a wholly new strategy. As an example, consider the case of Dometic, a Swedish company that was able to parlay a long series of successful adjacency moves in its core refrigeration business into a new and unexpected center of business gravity that completely transformed the business and its economics.

How Dometic Froze Out the Competition. In 1922, two Swedish engineering students named Carl Munters and Baltzar von Platen discovered an intriguing fact: using what is known as absorption technology, they built small, silent refrigeration units. A year later, Swedish company AB Electrolux purchased the rights to the two inventors' patents and began to produce absorption-based refrigerators. Whereas most household refrigerators use compressors driven by electric motors to generate cold, absorption refrigerators have no moving parts and don't need electricity, only a source of heat such as a propane tank. So they are particularly useful in places like boats or recreational vehicles, where electric current is hard to come by. The Electrolux unit responsible for absorption refrigerators was called Electrolux Leisure Appliances and was later to become the independent Dometic Group.

In 1973 Dometic was still small, with revenues of only kr80 million, and it was losing money. In 2005, after several waves of core redefinition, Dometic has grown to kr7.3 billion (about $1.2 billion). It is highly profitable, and it holds a leading position in all its core markets. Somehow in the intervening years, a small, seemingly hopeless old-line business metamorphosed into a money-making market leader.

The man who led Dometic's reinvention was Sven Stork. Initially tasked with fixing the ailing Electrolux product line, Stork went on to become president and CEO of Dometic after the company's sale to private equity firm EQT in 2001, and a few years later, became chairman of the board. (Dometic was sold again in 2005 to investment firm BC Partners, which appointed a new chairman; Stork is now senior adviser to the group.) Stork and his team introduced absorption refrigeration to the hotel minibar market, where the units' silent operation gave them an advantage over conventional refrigerators. That business grew rapidly, and Dometic acquired many of its competitors. Next, the team decided to expand its range of offerings for the recreational vehicle (RV) market, which was beginning to explode. The company's share in RV refrigerators, launched by Dometic in the 1950s, had grown over the years until Dometic captured nearly 100 percent of this segment. That gave the company a sustainable core from which to redefine itself.

Stork tells what happened next:

> We decided to make the RV into something that you could really live in. The idea was obvious to people who knew the customers, yet it took a while to convince the manufacturers and especially the rest of our own organization. So we began adding other related systems like air

conditioning, in 1983, and automated awnings, in 1986, to our product line, all sold through the same channel of installers and dealers. Gradually, through these moves, we began to build market power in the channel. So we added more product lines for even more functions to make an RV livable—cooking, lighting, sanitation systems, water purification, generators, and so on—until we had a complete system for RVs built up one step at a time, 60 percent through organic growth and 40 percent through acquisitions. Through twenty-nine acquisitions we built up repeatable skills at acquisition, something our competitors were definitely not doing and a capability that is core to us now.

Along the way, we decided to streamline the dealer business in the United States by taking out the distribution layer and going direct to the dealers, reducing the cost structure dramatically. We prepared for the risks like a military operation. It was a fantastic hit. We were the only company large enough to pull this off. It let us kill off competitors faster than they could come out of the bushes. We then focused on product-development speed, leaving the competitors another step behind us whenever we could. The skills that allowed higher development speed became a lasting part of our core.[5]

Now Dometic has 75 percent of the world market share for RV interior systems and leadership in the distribution channel. It is branching out into new adjacencies, notably other types of vehicles with "live in" characteristics, such as marine vessels and long-haul trucks. In a low-growth market for RVs, Dometic grew profitably at 10 percent per year from 1990 to 2005, an enviable record even in faster-growing markets. For comparison, only 7 percent of public companies in the G-7 economies achieved 5 percent real revenue growth, grew their profits, and earned their cost of capital. Dometic has met all these benchmarks in a market few would have noticed, from a starting point that looked bleak. By focusing on a kernel of promise in two successive moves to adjacent markets—absorption refrigeration and then RVs—it shifted out of its core and reinvented itself.

The basic pattern of Dometic's growth and redefinition is a textbook example, over many years, of the four key principles for success we've outlined: (1) gradualism during transformation, (2) the discovery and use of hidden assets, (3) underlying leadership economics central to the strategy, and (4) a move from one repeatable formula to another that is unique to the company. The first formula moved along the absorption refrigeration sector product-by-product (one of which was RVs); the second formula angled off, from the RV position into a sequence of interior components for RVs, eventually attaining leadership in that segment and its channels; and the third formula is now trying to replicate this strategic pattern for other interior systems, from boats to long-haul trucks.

The prominence of adjacency moves in redefining the strategy may not excite strategists who believe that companies need to reinvent their fundamental model. But many companies with serious problems in their core have counteracted the effects of growing strategic liabilities by building on hidden assets. Best of all, perhaps, is the occasional discovery that a series of past adjacency moves enables a new strategic direction, which then unlocks a series of repeated moves in a new direction (as in the case of Dometic). If you find a new strategy that has, at its center, a repeatable formula for driving further growth, you have the best of all worlds. Repeatability is at the heart of determining the outcome of some of the great competitive battles—Nike versus Reebok, Wal-Mart versus Kmart, and Starbucks versus your local coffee shop, to name only a few.

Platform 2: World-Class Support Organizations

Hollywood success stories are replete with examples of unknown actors who steal a scene and emerge as stars. A good example is Matt Damon's role in the movie *Mystic Pizza*. Damon appeared in one scene and had only a single line. But that short scene so caught the attention of audiences that it helped propel him to lead roles, stardom, and an Oscar.

We see the same phenomenon in many areas of life and so, too, in business. Some of the great business renewals have been triggered by functions or capabilities that were essential to support the core business and later assume center stage. Three of the most well documented business success stories follow this pattern: IBM, GE Capital, and American Airlines (Sabre). Their stories, summarized next, make my point on platforms for renewal.

IBM's Global Services Group, which in 2005 accounted for 35 percent of the entire company's profits, was once largely hidden from management's view. As the company struggled to compete in the fast-moving PC industry and the challenging mainframe and minicomputer markets, services weren't on anyone's radar screen. What began IBM's transformation was a "wholly owned IBM subsidiary named the Integrated Systems Services Corporation," recalls Louis Gerstner, the CEO who initiated the move. "ISSC was our services and network operations unit in the United States—a promising but minor part of IBM's portfolio. In fact it wasn't even a standalone business in IBM. It was a subunit of the salesforce."[6]

Gerstner and his team decided in 1993 to create a services business that would be independent of IBM's hardware divisions and, in fact, was allowed to recommend products from Hewlett-Packard or Sun or Microsoft if the situation called for it. In 1996 IBM spun out IBM Global Services as a separate business. From 1999 through 2001, as the company's hardware business stagnated at $37 billion in sales and then fell to $33 billion, the new services business began to carry the burden of corporate growth. By 2001 it had grown to $35 billion, larger than all of IBM's hardware business, and accounted for approximately two-thirds of the company's value. "Had the effort to build IBM Global Services failed," says Gerstner, "IBM, or at least my vision of IBM, would have failed with it." That says it all.

Similarly, the profit engine that drove more than 60 percent of General Electric's increase in value during the final decade of the

Jack Welch era was a neglected part of the portfolio named GE Capital. Founded in the 1930s to help Depression-era consumers purchase appliances, GE Capital grew slowly until the late 1980s as a support function for a wide range of customers in GE's equipment businesses. GE decided to develop a strategy for this support business and determine whether it was possible to make it much larger while maintaining its high profitability. The strategy worked.

From 1990 through 2000, GE Capital completed more than 170 acquisitions—more than one per month for more than a decade. By 2005, GE Capital had attained the remarkable size of $394 billion in assets, and accounted for 35 percent of GE's profits. Since this unit was discovered and brought into a leading role in the company, nearly two-thirds of GE's growth in shareholder value can be attributed to it.

A third example of a support function emerging in a central role is seen in airlines, an industry that has struggled for a long time to create economic value. The few gambits that have paid off have occurred through the discovery of a supporting function—for example, the reservation software and system in the case of American Airlines more than a decade ago, and the frequent-flier program in the case of Air Canada, spun off as a public company last year. In 2000, Sabre, American Airlines' reservation function, was sold to the public as a separate company; it promptly spawned a new core of its own, Travelocity, a leading Internet-based travel reservation business. In 2005 the combined businesses had revenues of $2.5 billion and today Sabre's market cap is more than half that of American Airlines. (For a time Sabre was even considerably more valuable than its parent.)

Air Canada's strategy is similar. It floated a series of support functions—including Aeroplan, its frequent-flier operation—on the Toronto Stock Exchange as separate economic entities under the umbrella of a holding company called ACE Aviation Holdings, Inc. The flotation of Aeroplan was 600 percent oversubscribed by investors and valued at $2 billion, many times the value of the airline itself.

Many of the hidden businesses that companies have used as broad platforms for renewal share one of two origins. Some are internal services developed to satisfy core customers in specialized situations, which then turn out to have broader appeal. IBM Global Services is one example. Others emerge from internal functional capabilities originally developed to strengthen the core; these capabilities then turn out to be the centerpiece of a new business. Sabre is an example of such a business.

The odds of success in all such cases are high. These hidden cores are relatively close-in moves, only one or two steps removed from the company's true core. They have proven themselves to be functional, maybe even profitable, within the core. Given those possibilities, it makes sense for most companies to place a high priority on the search for hidden cores, particularly companies in turbulent (or potentially turbulent) markets and businesses where new, unclaimed profit pools are forming.

Platform 3: Noncore Businesses and Orphan Product Lines

All acquirers dream that the next company they buy will prove to have massive untapped potential and will even be a catalyst in a transformation across the portfolio of their existing businesses. Only occasionally does this occur. But, like an art collector's discovery of a Rembrandt etching at a rummage sale, it does happen. Identifying the asset of the acquisition itself is obviously not as hard as seeing the promise of a support function or a combination of adjacency moves. But the full extent of an acquisition's untapped potential can be quite hidden, and so can some of the acquisition's deeper capabilities that provide that potential. In the case of the British retailer GUS, the full potential from two acquisitions—Experian, an information services firm, and Argos, a retail chain—proved over time to be greater than anticipated and acted as a catalyst in the restructuring of the entire company. In the years after the Argos acquisition, GUS sold off its original core Home Shopping business, and in 2006 demerged with its two remaining business (Burberry and Experian) as separate and healthy cores in their own right. Unlocking the potential of a hidden asset, Argos, was one of the keys to this transformation.

GUS: Migrating to a New Core. GUS (which stands for Great Universal Stores) began its life in 1900, the brainchild of Manchester residents Abraham and George Rose. The Roses saw that package delivery in the United Kingdom was more sophisticated and reliable than ever and so came up with the idea of starting a mail-order business, much like the fledgling Sears, Roebuck and Co. in the United States. Before long, the business, then known as Universal Stores, was the nation's largest catalog retailer. Its 440-page book came out twice a year. "From the pages of one catalogue," declares the company history, "a customer can clothe a family, [and] furnish and equip the entire household, all from the seclusion of a chair by the fireside." In 1930 the business was rechristened Great Universal Stores and listed on the London Stock Exchange. The arrival of a new chairman, Isaac Wolfson, "saw the start of a long period of expansion, checked only temporarily by the Second World War."[7]

"Expansion" describes the company's growth with typical British understatement. In fact GUS soon became the largest retail conglomerate in Europe. It bought Burberry Ltd., which produced the weatherproof cloth that had become standard equipment for the British Army and was used in the legendary raincoat. (Interestingly, we can look at the rejuvenation of Burberry as built on a set of hidden assets, such as the brand, which had fallen into disrepair.) GUS also bought the Lewis Group chain of stores in South Africa. It bought Waring & Gillow, a venerable furniture and furnishings store, and it bought other mail-order companies. All told, GUS came to own about eighty specialty retailers, most of them former family businesses whose owners sought liquidity. GUS added value through its distribution infrastructure and knowledge of retailing.

But nothing lasts forever, particularly in retail. By the mid-1990s David Wolfson, a nephew of Isaac's, had taken over the chairmanship. GUS's retailing and mail-order operations were now under threat from discounters and the proliferation of consumer credit. Still, one division—a small information-services business known as CCN—was doing well. Begun in 1980 to support GUS's mail-order operations, CCN had found external customers for its credit-rating services and was growing steadily. In 1996 GUS acquired Experian, a large North American information-services company, and merged it with CCN, keeping the Experian name. Later acquisitions and continued growth turned Experian into a global information-solutions company with significant business in the credit-rating market.

In 2000, a CCN founder named John Peace became CEO of GUS and began a transformation of the company's core. He exited many of GUS's other businesses, and spun off the Lewis Group and part of Burberry to shareholders. He then focused on making major improvements to GUS's three core businesses: Experian, the remaining holdings in Burberry, and the newly formed retail division comprising the GUS Home Shopping business and a recent acquisition, the Argos chain of retail stores. Within a short space of time, Peace and his team realized that the days of the old home-shopping format were numbered. They sold the business—the original core of the whole GUS group—for £600 million in 2003, in order to focus on realizing the full potential of Argos. They acquired a leading do-it-yourself (DIY) and home-furnishings retailer known as Homebase, melding it with Argos. They invested in growing the Internet channel, adding $2 billion in sales and turning Argos into one of the top three Internet retailers in the United Kingdom. Multichannel sales—stores, Internet, and telephone orders for store pickup—gave the company a big edge on its competitors.

Peace explains his thinking this way:

> We realized that the DIY, home enhancements, and furnishings market totaled £35 billion and was still very diffuse. Over 50 percent was in inefficient mom-and-pop stores that would be vulnerable to our advantages. So we invested further as we exited noncore assets. We purchased the retailer Homebase for around £900 million,

used our expertise in supply-chain and store logistics to improve it, and integrated it where appropriate with Argos. We also invested in increasing the product line of Argos from five thousand products to over seventeen thousand products today, which we felt we could manage because of our supply-chain expertise and ability to manage complex product lines, going back to the company's heritage in its core catalog business.

As we gained mass, we began to outsource from China our own lines of products, designed by use, such as a low-cost, light power drill suited perfectly to our DIY customer needs. We have created a virtuous cycle between all of these elements, fueled by cash from continued noncore divestitures. In 2000, the analysts imputed a value of £2 billion to the Argos retail group; just five years later, as the clear leader in the category, analysts are imputing to it a value of well over £5 billion.[8]

The results of this strategic redefinition have been impressive, and not only in the valuation of Argos. GUS's stock price rose 130 percent between 2000 and 2005 even though the FTSE 100 London stock index was down 30 percent. An April 2005 report from J.P. Morgan titled "Value in a Wretched Sector" said, "Operational and transformational performance has surprised us positively. GUS has consistently proven us wrong during its transformation."

How did GUS management know that the Argos retail business had the potential to underpin a redefinition of the group? John Peace cited three practical lessons, echoing the sentiments of managers in other case examples we studied. "The first key," he said, "was to think like a private investor or venture capitalist with regard to the full potential of the asset, to bring a much more aggressive analytical perspective to bear on the valuation of the business." For instance, a number of product categories that were core to Argos competed in relatively fragmented markets, against mom-and-pop operations. Managers thought that these stores could be beaten on price by an aggressive competitor doing global sourcing and using sophisticated replenishment technology to expand the product line. Moreover, when the company looked more closely, it saw that the full market size—$35 billion—was much larger than it had imagined. Then it was a matter of taking a mind-set toward what was possible that was much different from the incremental budget-setting process of the past.

A second lesson emphasized by Peace was the need to change key managers, installing people who saw the potential of Argos, believed in the expanded vision, and had the skills to pursue it. The third element was a new performance-based pay system, with new metrics tied to the success of the growth strategy. The process ignited the company, and it took off.

The transformation of GUS is a case of seeing an entire business in a different light, with greater potential than previously recognized, and of a reconstituted management team's assault on that potential—with dramatic results.

Orphan Products: From Lost to Found. Instead of a business, the undervalued platform may be a product line. For instance, Arm & Hammer baking soda has been taken from a relatively stale product line into the profit and growth engine for Church & Dwight. Robert Davies III, the CEO who led the charge, said at the start of the renewal, "I looked at those yellow boxes of baking soda and I said there's 10, 15, 20 new products inside that box that just need to come tumbling out and be formulated and packaged."[9]

Or the platform might be a set of activities that is literally a by-product of the core product line. For instance, years from now, it is possible that we will look back on the history of De Beers and see enormous value in Element Six, a business unit formed around De Beers's entry in the 1950s into, and eventual technical leadership in, synthetic industrial diamonds. Beyond their qualities as a gemstone, diamonds have remarkable physical properties, such as the highest level of biological inertness (nonreactivity) of any known material, the highest resistance to thermal shock, and the greatest degree of hardness. These and other properties could make synthetic industrial diamonds superior alternatives for a range of new applications, from coating mining machinery parts to creating pathways for targeting lasers, to forming substrate for semiconductors, to building the speaker domes of the highest-end audio systems. It is too early to say how this market will evolve, but it is the type of hidden core, going back to research started more than forty years ago by De Beers, that can suddenly emerge as central to creating value in the future.

Another platform might be orphan products scattered throughout a company waiting to be collected in one place to transform their potential and create new growth. Nestlé, which at $69 billion in revenues is the largest food and nutrition company in the world, and at one hundred forty years is also one of the oldest, offers a good illustration. Under CEO Peter Brabeck, who took over in 1997, Nestlé has grown organically at 5.7 percent and, with acquisitions, at 7 percent in an industry that is growing at about half that rate. Nestlé, as a whole, is not a candidate for redefinition. However, even the largest companies must periodically look at redefining parts of their business to take advantage of nearby untapped profit pools. Nestlé recognized that one of the largest such profit pools was for food and drink consumed outside the home—from vending machines, in cafeterias and restaurants, and even at work.

When Nestlé examined more closely its connection to this gigantic market, it discovered that it was already one of the largest participants in the food service business, with slightly less than 10 percent of its sales serving that market: Nescafé sold through vending machines, Stouffer's frozen meals packaged for service outside the home, and a series of Nestlé brands for restaurant professionals. As a result, Nestlé collected this set of service businesses under one umbrella and developed a unified strategy to participate in food services through a new multibillion-dollar business assembled from a collection of noncore products and services.

Detecting Undervalued Business Platforms

There is no guarantee, of course, that these types of hidden assets exist in a given company, nor that they will provide the linchpin to future strategy. However, the world is filled with examples of companies that did not fully value their hidden assets and learned about it too late. A classic example is the stream of developments by Xerox PARC in the 1980s. These products included many of the key technologies for small printers that eventually captured much of the profit pool (at the hands of competitors like Hewlett-Packard, the leader in printers) and eroded traditional xerography.[10] One study calculated that the value of the companies spawned from technologies

Detecting Undervalued Business Platforms

Our case analysis and a review of the Bain case archives highlight a series of six indicators, or predictors, of possible hidden assets:

- *Importance to core customers.* You may be dragged into a business or adjacency by customer requests, as with IBM Global Services. This case demonstrates that customer demand is a predictor of latent value.

- *Unusual ability to grow profitably despite inattention.* GE Capital is the quintessential example. The lesson: comb through your portfolio for pockets of profitable growth in areas that have not received focused attention, and ask why that is.

- *Prosperity in the midst of a large and growing profit pool.* This is a trickier one to recognize because it requires a certain knowledge of external profit pools and business boundaries. But certainly the iPod story falls into this category.

and small businesses that Xerox did not fully value now exceeds the value of the former parent by a significant amount.

Bain & Company surveys routinely show that two out of three senior executives do not believe that their organizations are operating at close to full potential in their primary cores. If that is true, it must be more so for secondary businesses, support functions, or clusters of adjacencies. Often, companies have entered these positions more for their short-term growth potential than for their long-term strategic value. But values change over time. Occasionally these hidden assets are transformational, the centerpiece of a new strategy. But sometimes they are simply overlooked or abandoned opportunities that would strengthen the core and buy time for a structural solution.

- *Robust positions of leadership (no matter how small).*
  This was certainly the case for the life-sciences products of PerkinElmer, as recognized by Tony White and his team.

- *Capabilities that demonstrate world-class excellence.* This is the case in the De Beers independent division Element Six, which is using the company's world-class level of knowledge regarding synthetic industrial diamonds as a platform to spawn a range of new businesses.

- *Diffuse, but similar, activities across business units that might form the core of a new business.* Nestlé did this in food services (catering, cafeterias, etc.) and nutritional health (health foods, medically constituted nutritional products), creating two new multibillion-dollar cores that are profitable, growing, and have strong competitive positions.

Few hidden assets will meet these requirements, and the undervalued assets that emerge may hold only limited potential. However, it is possible to discover that the answer to strategic redefinition was right in front of you all along.

Using Hidden Assets

The discovery of a treasure trove of hidden assets does not, on its own, solve the problem with which we started this book: finding and implementing the right new strategy when your success formula is approaching a limit. When you gain greater comprehension of underutilized assets, however, you gain a toolkit and access to new ideas that expand the range of practical strategic options. Even partial success might provide ways to defer or dilute the impending growth gap and buy time to explore new options.

The management team that is entering a period of questioning and strategic self-appraisal should ask the following questions:

- What are my hidden assets (noncore businesses, support functions, or adjacencies)?

- What are their links to the current core? How important are they?

- Do I really understand the full stand-alone potential of these assets?

- What are the known strategic options that could put these assets to better use?

- Does greater understanding of these assets suggest new options?

- What other ingredients are needed for these new options? Where would we get them?

In chapter 4 we turn to the second of the three types of hidden assets: those that emanate from the complex web of customer relationships that most companies build over the years.

4

Untapped Customer Insights

Customer is the most fundamental word in business. Without customers there is no business and no need for it. When you stop understanding your customers, you stop understanding your own business. Redefining the basic customer relationship at the heart of your business model is tantamount to tampering with the heart of your economics. But sometimes it must be done. Nine of the twenty-five more in-depth case studies of strategic redefinition or renewal in this book—or nearly two-fifths—entailed moving to a next-generation customer model.

In our Growth Survey, 65 percent of executives indicated that they would have to change their customer model to maintain their growth. When we asked them about the most important capabilities that they could add to their business to trigger a new wave of growth, they put "capabilities to understand our core customer more deeply" at the top of the list. Seventy-four percent of those same executives said that their customer data was becoming obsolete faster than ever, meaning that they were likely to understand their customers less well in the future.

One striking measure of this emerges from work we have done on the gap between customer perceptions and supplier perceptions.

We asked a large sample of managers how differentiated (in the product or the quality of its delivery) they thought they were in serving their clients with their core product offering; 80 percent said "very differentiated." By contrast, a similar sample of their customers indicated that only about 8 percent felt that their suppliers were highly differentiated.

This sort of perception gap suggests that companies are likely to react too slowly to circumstances that may be eroding their customer franchise, or they may realize too late that they need to re-examine the fundamentals of their customer model. This research points to the critical importance of redefining how you serve your customers.

In our consulting work, we observe that companies' level of knowledge and awareness about customers varies greatly, ranging from the most outdated to the most incisive (the latter received using the Internet in real time). The ability to capture direct, fast, high-quality customer feedback is one of the remaining true competitive advantages—and in some industries, maybe the ultimate edge.

I recently participated in a series of business seminars in which our team administered an online survey to the participants. All were from strong, even leading, businesses. Yet the average rate of agreement to the question "Do you agree with the following statement: We understand our customers?" was less than 25 percent. That says it all.

We recently examined the results of 105 studies on changes in strategic direction done by Bain & Company for our clients around the world. In half the cases, our teams reported that the answer was to fundamentally change a key element of the customer model or even the choice of core customer.

This chapter examines three hidden customer assets that were central in the cases of strategic renewal. The first is the undervalued customer segment. You discover these customers when you realize that you possess a potential competitive advantage you've neglected because you haven't looked at aggregating, or disaggregating, customers in the right way.

The second type of hidden customer asset is a position of untapped influence over a specific group of customers. Often, you gain such a position because you enjoy the trust of your customers. The De Beers example that began this book illustrates this type of unexploited asset. The third form of hidden asset is proprietary data or information that can be used to alter, deepen, or broaden the customer relationship.

The remarkable transformation of Harman International illustrates the power of a newly discovered customer segment. This high-end audio equipment company renewed itself in dramatic fashion by focusing on a specific customer segment (automotive OEMs) as well as by associating Harman's premium brands in audio, Harman/Kardon, JBL, Mark Levinson and Infinity, with the invention of a new type of product—infotainment systems. This change in customer strategy led to ten years of profitable growth. It took Harman from strategic stasis and impending crisis to a nearly forty-fold increase in market value.

The Transformation of Harman International

Founded in 1953 by Sidney Harman and Bernard Kardon to package amplifiers and tuners in a single unit called a receiver, Harman International (then known as Harman-Kardon) long occupied a place of pride in the market for high-quality audio equipment. Throughout its storied history, Harman's equipment processed the signals for many of the definitive sound-recording events in music. Indeed, its JBL line of speakers was the sound system at the legendary 1969 Woodstock music festival, and the company's professional audio division now has leading market share in top concert halls around the world. Harman International refers to itself as a "company of listeners." As its recent metamorphosis suggests, this might refer both to live musicians and to the drumbeats of the marketplace.

By 1993, however, Harman had lost its growth rhythm. It had revenues of $600 million, but its profits hovered close to zero and market value was only $132 million. Sidney Harman, who had left the company to serve as Deputy Secretary of Commerce, returned as CEO to try to rejuvenate the company. Harman and his team soon embarked on a new course, building on a longtime platform that had not been fully exploited: the company's position as a provider of audio equipment to the automotive original equipment manufacturer (OEM) segment. In 1992, the low point for Harman International, the auto OEM segment constituted less than 10 percent of the company, and even less of its profitability. Today, this formerly unexploited asset is the growth and profit engine of the company, accounting for 75 percent of revenues, more than 90 percent of profits, and nearly 100 percent of profitable growth over that period.

Harman's long history has been one of cycling around its three segments—consumer, professional, and automotive—with a different one taking center stage across successive decades. Today, based largely on its success in selling systems to the automotive market, Harman's market value has increased by forty times in twelve years; revenues have climbed by five times (to $3.2 billion); and pretax profits have risen to $391 million, generating a 23 percent return on equity. This virtuoso performance is remarkable, especially for a small company competing in an industry of giants, all of them competing intensely at the intersection of two of the most competitive markets in the world: consumer electronics and automotive OEM supply.

Harman's strongest asset has always been its position as the highest-quality producer of sound systems, through its own technology and by accumulating a series of small, specialized audiophile companies along the way. At its low point in the early 1990s, Harman's hidden asset was its position in automotive. In 1995, the company purchased Becker, a German company that had produced the Becker autophon, the first car radio, in 1948 and in 1996 had introduced the first fully digital fiber-optic car radio. Yet despite Becker's history, when Harman International purchased the company it was in trouble and unprofitable due to competition from Japanese manufacturers. Sidney Harman describes what happened:

> Our entry into the OEM business occurred almost twenty years ago when we persuaded Jack Eby, a well-placed, creative, and uncharacteristically daring automotive executive at Ford, that the Ford Company should follow his instinct. That instinct was to offer a truly high-quality music reproduction system as an option in the car. It would, he believed, be appealing to a fairly large constituency. That constituency, we agreed, was of people who loved music, spent an increasing amount of time in the car, and had begun to think of it as something of a sanctuary. When Ford had success with our JBL-branded system, we, as reasonable business folk, marketed that success to other automakers.
>
> Then, ten years ago, we acquired the once notable Becker radio company in Germany. That company had, for half a century, been the sole maker of radios for Mercedes-Benz, who had treated Becker as family. The absence of strict control and cost awareness represented no problem when Becker had a grand sponsor, but when Japanese automakers began to make progress, Mercedes awakened to the fact that it needed to function more professionally—and it did. Unfortunately, Becker could not follow suit and fell into terrible disarray.
>
> We acquired it after a competition among nearly a dozen firms. I am convinced that not one of us had a serious fix either on the depth of Becker's difficulties or on its opportunities. Likely each of us thought, "There must be a pony in that barn."
>
> Shortly after our acquisition, I visited the Becker plant in Germany—a traditional early visit by "the old man" to sprinkle proverbial holy water. There, three very creative

(and I suspect slightly desperate) engineers had laid out a display for me. On an enormous table, they had placed a collection of boxes representing the analog hardware necessary to offer a collection of functions in the auto-mobile (music, video, voice-activated telephone, Internet access, navigation, climate control, et cetera). Atop the collection of simulated hardware boxes, they had placed the cable and harnessing necessary to interconnect all that stuff. It was overwhelming, and manifestly imprac-tical for installation in a car. It represented too much weight, too much cost, and too much real estate. On another table approximately the size of a small desk, they had placed the boxes representing a digital expression of the same system. Atop that assembly, they had placed what appeared to be a single strand of spaghetti. It was the optical bus, which, in effect, replaced all that wiring and harnessing. One would have been an idiot not to see the future. That led us to commit the resources necessary to build a serious software/digital R&D resource. That strategy has led to the dominant role the company plays in the design and manufacture of what has been identi-fied as the automotive infotainment system—essentially the central nervous system of the automobile. Today we are the major supplier to such firms as Mercedes, BMW, Porsche, Audi, Chrysler, and Hyundai.[1]

Along the way, Harman added further capabilities to stay ahead in the race for leadership in the infotainment system category. Essen-tially it had created this category from its deep base of audio engi-neering, its beachhead in OEM sales, and its additional truly hidden asset (hidden in the sense of its full potential) in the acquisition of Becker.

How did Harman International pull this off as a smaller player in the notoriously competitive consumer electronics business through a strategy of selling to the equally competitive automotive suppliers? The answer lies in a combination of things. One is a unique set of hidden assets that it recognized (the Becker position and the high-end brand appeal) and the ability to use the knowledge from its consumer and professional (soundstage) business in developing the highest-quality products.

The second element was Harman's decision to build on its strength, going first after the top of the market, as Harman describes:

> An industry enthralled with tonnage is an industry headed over the cliff. We decided to focus on the highest-quality product that appealed to real consumer need and make it as simple as we could. As a result, the automotive OEM companies sometimes made more profit on the sound system than on the rest of the car, and part of it was the premium for the consumer endorsement of the best high-fidelity system, which we represented. Those systems were branded and nothing else was. I bought a BMW and found one beautiful BMW logo on the steering wheel and nine elsewhere for Harman/Kardon in the car. I like that ratio. We can afford to stay loyal to the view that we will do margin, not tonnage.

A third factor was Harman's good fortune in the advance of technology and its ability to innovate. By recognizing the convergence of electronic information capabilities for the car and the unique level of customer trust and access in the brand (another hidden asset), Harman was well positioned to integrate these new services into its audio systems, including over time other devices such as cell phones, video, and navigation.

This chapter examines the way hidden customer assets can be used to reshape a strategy by addressing the following questions. What are the main forms of hidden assets, and how can they be the linchpin of renewal? What are the best ways to identify hidden assets and to recognize the range of options that they enable? From our research, what are some of the pitfalls and practical considerations when you change the customer model?

Unexploited Customer Segments

A typical customer base contains thousands, even tens of thousands, of customers—businesses, consumers, and distributors. There are nearly infinite ways that you can view a complex customer base built over time. Yet it's worthwhile to take the time to figure out the patterns that best explain the underlying causes of purchase behaviors and basic needs. In some cases, this kind of study can reveal segments of great strength or great potential, now lost in the haze of commerce, on which you can build a coherent strategy.

The lenses that you use to view the world affect everything, including how you analyze your customers. Changing those lenses can alter your sense of what is possible, the limits you face, the threats around you, and even your core. Often your perception of reality is as important in shaping your actions and your future as reality itself. When these mental maps change, the world is never again the same to you.

Anton van Leeuwenhoek developed a set of lenses—the first microscope—which allowed people to view the world in a new way. He grew up in Delft, the Netherlands, as the son of a basket maker. During his ninety years, he left his town only twice, and then only briefly. Yet his invention opened an undiscovered frontier that was as vast, and as profound in its implications, as the frontiers explored at great expense by the ocean voyages of Columbus and Magellan or the astronomical observations of Galileo. In 1674 Leeuwenhoek examined a drop of lake water and found "very many small animalcules." He created a superthin tube of glass containing a single drop of this water and set it on a system of silver springs with thirty divisions so that he could use his new instrument to view minute slices of that drop. He produced signed written testimonials from visitors to his shop that he had seen thousands of living organisms in one-thirtieth of a drop of water.[2] Leeuwenhoek's lenses redefined the boundaries of many fields, from microbiology to botany and crystallography.

Seeing the world differently, correctly, and early enough is the precursor to the successful redefinition of a company. This is especially true in the quest to look at an established customer base in different ways, searching for patterns of behavior and new ways to aggregate, or disaggregate, customers. What, specifically, should you look for? Our cases highlight three types of hidden segments that can become the fulcrum of a new strategy:

- New, emerging segments with attractive profit pool characteristics

- Historic core segments whose potential and competitive position have been forgotten

- Narrow, vertical niches that can be identified one by one, often with a repeatable formula that can propel strategy and competitive advantage in the future

Harman is an example of redefinition based on a new customer segment, in this case consumers of high-end infotainment. The next example, Autodesk, illustrates the other types of hidden segments.

Autodesk: Rediscovering Customer Segments

Autodesk's history is a roller-coaster ride: rise, fall, and renewal. Each step was shaped by a different view of customer segmentation.

Autodesk began its life in Marin County, California, in 1982. This PC-focused software start-up of sixteen people was founded by John Walker. In his first open letter to employees on January 19 of that year, Walker showed an uncannily accurate vision of the future:

> We're entering a marketplace which is expanding at an unbelievable rate. Wander through any office tower in downtown San Francisco and look at how many desks have computers on them. Say, less than 1%. In five years or so, 80% to 100% of those desks are going to have computers on them, and those computers will be running

programs that have not been written yet. In less than six weeks, over 100,000 IBM personal computers have been sold. There is little or no serious application software for that machine at present . . . and how many will they sell in the next five years. . . ?[3]

Despite this prescience, the product that ultimately fueled the growth and success of the company over the next twenty-five years—computer-aided design software for architects and engineers—was an afterthought, a subordinate product idea in the company's original suite of offerings.

Four years later, Walker reflected to a West Coast audience:

> In 1982, my company started selling a computer aided drafting and design program which ran on PCs. The conventional wisdom, as represented by those venture capitalists and analysts we could get to talk to us was:
>
> 1. You can't do CAD on a PC.
>
> 2. Even if you could, no serious user would buy it.
>
> 3. Computer dealers can't sell CAD systems.
>
> Well, we didn't have anything else to do, so we just went ahead and tried anyway. To date [1986], we've sold in excess of forty thousand CAD packages for PCs. To put this number in perspective, it is on the order of twice the number of workstations of the most widely used mainframe CAD system.[4]

Over its first decade, Autodesk grew to become the fifth-largest software company in the world. After its IPO stock price expanded tenfold, it became synonymous with 2-D computer-aided design. For ten years, the industry named its AutoCAD software a best product, disproving a 1985 *BusinessWeek* article that referred to the company as "the high-tech issue that may not fly."[5] In a development that proves how unknowable business can be, in 1986 and 1987,

BusinessWeek featured Autodesk as the "Hot Growth Company of the Year."[6]

Yet during the Internet bubble of the late 1990s, Autodesk, like many others, took some wrong turns. It abandoned its strategy of pursuing deep, technical applications software for its engineering design customers sold through the indirect channel (resellers and retailers). Instead, it began broadening its reach into new forms of services and new direct channels, striving to become an Internet company. CEO Carl Bass explains:

> The company had adopted a Hail Mary strategy, trying lots of new and different things, often throwing business analysis and [proven] practices to the wind. We told our indirect channel partners who had helped us build the company in the earlier years that we were going to move 40 percent of our business to a direct channel and 20 percent on the Web and eat into the 80 percent of the business we were doing through them. We started to move farther and farther from our core in the hope of becoming an Internet company of some kind. We reduced our focus on our design tools and began to move into more and more vectors that moved us farther and farther from our strength. As a result, our revenues even declined for a period of time, dropping back below $1 billion. This was done under an umbrella strategy that we called life cycle management.
>
> A competitor, Parametric Technology, had built a $1.1 billion CAD business and followed a similar path. Today [2005] that company has declined in revenues to $.7 billion.[7]

Autodesk had to change, and it did so through a series of new strategic initiatives that hinged on several hidden customer assets. First, the company determined that the indirect channel was a hidden asset that it had not fully appreciated and, as a result, returned to it with a vengeance. Autodesk began to reinvest in its two thousand channel partners. As Bass says, "We stopped competing with them. We treated them like our own salesforce and invested in basic training. We pruned down to the best ones and invested alongside these small mom-and-pop businesses."

Second, the management team shifted its focus to deep and narrow vertical segments of the specialized market of applications engineers. The new strategy was to drill deeply rather than tunnel broadly, a significant change in direction.

Third, the Autodesk team realized that it had a hidden asset in the form of abundant 3-D technology. With reinvestment, it could use this technology to produce modeling and simulation software for each of its target customer segments. Fourth, Autodesk changed its management team to implement the new strategy. Today, only 25 percent of the top fifty managers remain. Finally, Autodesk changed to a subscription model for software upgrades, migration packages from 2-D to 3-D, and add-ons.

Each of these actions is a critical, integrated component of the revenue model in a software business. To be successful, Autodesk adopted approaches seen in parallel software businesses. And they worked.

Since implementing the new strategy—rebuilding on formerly underused assets in the core—the company has renewed its performance. The stock price, which had declined to $6 per share in 2002, has increased six times in four years, to $36 per share. Revenues are growing at 16 percent, more than double those of the enterprise software industry; they have now reached more than $1.5 billion. Margins have reached 24 percent and are continuing to increase, driving return on equity to a stellar 46 percent. The company, whose 3-D software was used to model King Kong in the movie of the same name, is again marauding through its industry, with the power of its redefined strategy.

In our research, the types of segmentation insights that propelled Autodesk to redefine its strategy have proven to be the lenses that have repeatedly uncovered opportunities beneath the surface of business as usual. One distributor's segmentation efforts revealed that its core customer amounted to a collection of businesses that made numerous unplanned purchases—at best, an unpredictable platform for growth. As a result, the distributor took a series of initiatives to help these erratic customers with their inventory management and thereby smooth out their demand. At the same time, the distributor shifted its strategy to find a way to serve customers whose demand was more predictable.

Consider another instance: a company that sold hospital supplies, with high market share in intensive care units. The company found that the most important determinant of sales was not the level of care in the hospital but instead subtle combinations of patient attributes. The company segmented the patient population and launched a strategy that was built on microsegments of clinical characteristics.

In a third instance, a retailer of pet supplies discovered that the most profitable potential customers were those with certain types of pets and living situations that led them to purchase a great many pet services (grooming, housing, medical care). The company segmented the owner and pet populations and built a strategy that shifted its focus from pet supplies to a broader set of pet products and services. In so doing, it shifted from competing in a true dog-eat-dog commodity world to providing a unique offering with better profit potential to previously hidden customer segments—a win on two counts.

A profitable customer segment may emerge when managers redefine how they serve a certain type of customer, as in the case of the pet company. But it can also involve finding new ways to disaggregate existing segments into microsegments, or even segments of one. I mention elsewhere in the book Nike's ability in some of its markets to change the customer game by creating more targeted and segmented products than ever. One example is the company's entry into the soccer market in Europe a number of years ago; after only a few years, it's catching up with Adidas in that German company's core sports market. One technique involved refined segmentation of soccer balls into balls for various surfaces and conditions (dirt, hard surfaces, grass, even night conditions), and soccer shoes tailored by position and style of play.

An even more extreme form of disaggregation is practiced by a number of Internet companies such as Amazon.com, which has, through its software, tailored customers' Web pages to previously chosen interests and purchasing patterns, recommending products and ideas. Other companies might find that their customer data, easily and broadly collected by the Internet, now holds insights that can point the way to transforming their selling model. All these cases, and dozens more that our team has identified, show how new insights about unrecognized customer segments, and their economic characteristics, have led to redefined strategies and improved performance.

The Consequences of Segment Blindness

Failure to understand segmentation is a form of failure to understand your customers. It can pass unnoticed, a missed opportunity, but it can be much more costly.

If competitors recognize distinct customer segments that can be attacked with very different strategies—and your company doesn't—you can be vulnerable to a pincer movement from competitors, which can pick off your customers with more focused offerings. A successful example is global bank ING, which launched a low-cost, direct, Internet-based offering called ING Direct. This highly focused targeting of Web-savvy, self-sufficient customers has helped the bank gain rapid market share against competitors that did not see this emerging segmentation.

Failure to recognize segmentation, even in the absence of competitive attack, can also be a form of inefficiency. It means that you are significantly overserving some segments and underserving others, wasting resources that could be put to better use. This is a mismatch that competitors can exploit.

Incorrect segmentation means that you probably do not understand your market position. The stall-out at Autodesk was attributable, in part, to a failure to see the power of vertical application segments beneath the surface of the general architect and large categories of design engineers. Based on the potential of vertical segmentation, CEO Carl Bass says that the company can double in size to $3 billion.

Finally, segment blindness means you probably do not understand your profit pool or where you really make money. The turnaround of one air carrier, El Salvador–based TACA, came after the carrier recognized it held a strong, profitable advantage in helping a specific type of customer: natives of Central America shuttling back and forth to visit relatives and even returning their remains to their homeland after death. These customers counted on TACA for an extremely important service, both emotionally and economically, and TACA refocused on providing it with great care.

What are some of the signs that hidden segments, with true strategic implications, might exist unrecognized in your business? My experience, and our research, reveals a few clear indicators. The first occurs when the key measure of customer loyalty in your business varies widely among customers, and you do not know why. (One such indicator is Net Promoter Scores, the percentage of customers who would enthusiastically recommend your products and services to friends, minus the percentage who would not. This measure, discussed earlier in chapter 2, has earned a rapidly increasing following.)[8] This suggests that there are groups of customers you do not understand in basic ways.

Another indicator is an unexplained loss in market share in part of your historic customer base, suggesting that there is a distinct segment of customers being suddenly underserved (or better served elsewhere). A third indicator occurs when you or your largest competitor has not changed customer segment strategies for a long time. If this is true in a dynamic industry, perhaps you understand neither your customers nor their profitability. That constitutes a big opportunity to refocus.

Undervalued Customer Influence and Access

The De Beers example shows how a century-old company can turn its strategy around by taking a different view of its customer base. In a sparkling performance to be sure, De Beers increased the value of its diamond business from $1 billion to more than $9 billion in two years. If you probe deeply, you inevitably conclude that underlying De Beers's ability to change was its customers' trust, the company's brand power, its association with the highest-quality natural diamonds, and the extraordinary level of knowledge it had of its distributors. All these elements constitute an underused asset that gave De Beers more access and influence than it had realized.

Throughout our case studies of strategic redefinition, we saw versions of this pattern. A company had built up, over the years, access and knowledge of its customers at a deep level that it had not taken full advantage of, to the detriment of customers as well as the supplier. The case of Hyperion Solutions illustrates the strategic potential of such hidden power and influence.

Hyperion Solutions: A Case of Undervalued Influence

In the summer of 2001, the managers of Hyperion Solutions were sitting, tense and apprehensive, in a conference room in The Fairmont San Francisco, symbolically consuming nothing but bread and water. In the background, somber dinner music played: Elton John's "Funeral for a Friend." The company—which once had more than 50 percent penetration of the *Fortune* 100 companies in its core software product for financial consolidation—was in trouble, and management was acknowledging its resolve to reignite the profitable growth it had once enjoyed.

The previously high-flying company had suddenly stalled out. Its growth trajectory was flat, its 2001 profits had been negative, and its market value had dropped to about $500 million on revenues of

$528 million. Operations were in shambles, and the situation was worsened by a difficult merger integration. The company's new CEO, Jeff Rodek, states, "Following the merger, mass defections were going on. The company was not at risk of going bankrupt, but definitely at risk of becoming irrelevant."[9] Hyperion was also realizing that an unfocused strategy compounded its operational problems.

In the days and months that followed, Rodek and his team overhauled the company and its strategy. They concentrated first on stabilizing the base business. They eliminated troubled product lines, downsized facilities, agreed on four metrics that would define progress in the company, and focused immediately on improving execution of the basics (such as reducing days of receivables outstanding, which had ballooned to 106).

The larger strategic questions that loomed before them were profound. Question: was the client-server architecture and the Essbase OLAP technology behind the company's flagship product, business performance management (BPM) software, adequate for the future? Answer: no, Hyperion's customers were entering BPM through queries of relational databases. Rodek says of that time, "We found that the world was not a cube, but round. The need to build around relational databases was virtually a religious change for us." Question: would the company at least have the right capabilities after it finished the operational fix? Answer: no, Hyperion needed to have deep and highly specialized capabilities in query and business intelligence in order to rebuild its applications software and be competitive. Question: was the company set up to sell the way customers would want to buy in the future? Answer: not really. Customers were buying data software first, then reporting software, then customer applications and packaging, and then an integrated suite. The questions went on, casting doubt on every element of the company's strategy.

The bulk of spending in the market was shifting toward purchasing software as a suite and vendor consolidation, neither of which Hyperion was fully ready for. Moreover, the most attractive form of sale was indirect: software packages put together by system integrators. These companies brought the Hyperion product into the largest transactions and worked to tailor their solutions to valuable niche markets. These broad ecosystems of partners were gaining importance in software and technology companies, and Hyperion had to revise its selling priorities to become a more complete participant in that process. Addressing these questions required further major changes in the basic model: change in the software platform and architecture, change in the selling proposition to customers, and change in the internal capabilities. It was a lot to do.

Yet Hyperion accomplished its mission. The business stabilized operationally following intense focus on executing the basics, changes in the team, and restructuring of communication and rewards based on the four key metrics. Its leadership set a new strategy to build a full suite of financial and consolidation products, develop capabilities to report and analyze relational databases, and revamp the selling and service model to customer needs.

Looking back, we can see one hidden asset that was pivotal in the company's effort to make the new strategy work and stick. It was the strength of a specific customer franchise—corporate finance departments—that had grown to rely on Hyperion software for financial consolidation and SEC reporting. Rodek says, "We totally underestimated the power of the asset we had built in the finance department and how much they relied upon us for this very technical and sensitive part of their job."

The results were fast and impressive. Hyperion's market value reached $2 billion, a fourfold improvement in four years. Margins improved 20 points (to 16 percent), and the changes Hyperion made in its customer model increased the customer base from six thousand to more than twelve thousand companies, at the same time extending its leadership position in the BPM segment. The combination of operational restructuring and a full strategic redefinition was essential. Neither initiative on its own would have come close to solving the immediate problem and generating a renewed level of performance.

Untapped Customer Data and Information

Suppose you were a medical device company that suddenly discovered that you had been collecting, and could further collect, predictive data on when the device would fail and on the health of customers. You would have the ingredients, as some health care companies are now discovering, to change your model and the game in your industry.

Or suppose you were in the package delivery business and had become the first to track every package instantly (as UPS and FedEx do). You would have a powerful game-changing tool. Or suppose you were in the sports equipment business and you could collect performance data on athletes that could be linked to programs to improve athletic performance (as Nike is pursuing). Or suppose you could use purchase data to predict with great accuracy, and the greatest odds of success, which products or services your customers would want to buy (as Wal-Mart and Amazon.com have done in different ways).

All these ways of knowing your customers would, for a time, let you change the customer model and redefine your relationship with your core customer. With companies having seemingly unlimited data storage capacity and with the Internet and wireless technology vastly expanding what can be collected, information and IT services can become the epicenter of strategic renewal.

The Redefinition of American Express

One company that I have used in past writing and research is American Express. It epitomizes the issues and dangers encountered at each phase of the focus-expand-redefine cycle.

The ill-starred expansion of American Express in the 1980s was an effort for the company to become a financial supermarket, as chronicled in *Beyond the Core*. American Express wound up with an inflated cost structure as a result of bundling together numerous businesses and trying to cross-sell their services. It didn't work. The market's negative reaction to American Express's unfulfilled vision, and its collapse in earnings, led to a loss of investor confidence, and a steep drop in stock price. From 1989 to 1990, American Express lost 40 percent of its market value, and takeover rumors swirled around the company. In 1993, the company installed a new management team: Harvey Golub and Ken Chenault. They acted quickly to eliminate $2 billion in costs and refocus the company on the core businesses that directly supported the American Express brand. They rallied the organization around three operating principles: offer superior value to all customer groups, achieve best-in-class economics, and support the American Express brand in all activities. In the process, they divested many businesses that had been acquired as part of the failed strategy of the prior decade.

But could a pared-down and restructured American Express make for a healthy company? American Express's core charge-card business enjoyed a leading position with corporate customers, but the business was geared almost entirely to travel expenditures. These expenditures account for only a few percent of a typical corporation's costs and 3 percent of the average personal budget, but they accounted for more than 70 percent of the purchases put on the company's green, gold, and platinum charge cards in 1993. The entire business was geared to this category of purchase (travel and entertainment) and specific kinds of customers (business accounts and individual business travelers).

Meanwhile, American Express's primary competitors—Visa and MasterCard—served a full range of consumers and businesses and their full range of expenditures. Clearly, if American Express couldn't redefine its business, it would be painted into an increasingly small and unsustainable corner by its broad-based competition. The question was how to effect this redefinition. Chenault describes how the management team began a long series of moves to diversify into different kinds of card spending, customize products, expand merchant acceptance and introduce rewards for more specific customer segments. Those changes redefined the core of the company:

We began by redefining the distinctive segments of high-spending customers, redirecting our product development efforts to address each segment one by one, offering specific, tailored card products for each of them, and greatly expanding the range of goods and services customers could purchase using American Express products. We redirected every internal process towards an end-to-end customer relationship approach, rather than a series of disconnected activities. We found, looking at the business in this new way, that we had two hundred steps in product development, with multiple handoffs, and it was often hard to identify one single person who was ultimately responsible for decisions. We could not even answer the question of what the product-development cycle time was. We now have it down to a handful of steps in an integrated process with clear lines of responsibility. As a result, development of a new product, which used to take twelve to twenty-four months, now takes one to three months. We used to have only three customer segments: small business, large business, and business travelers. We now track and study several hundred key segments. We have completely redesigned incentives around the customer at every level of the organization.

When we began the process, about 70 percent of card spending was travel and entertainment. Now it is down to about 30 percent, with retail and everyday spending making up 70 percent. That's a far better reflection of how our customers actually spend their money. We have become focused outwards, not inwards.[10]

In short, American Express has transformed its core in its structure, internal processes, mind-set, compensation, the language it uses to describe itself, and economic returns.

At the same time, Chenault reinforced the importance of superior customer service, a traditional strength of the company. "More products can easily add more complexity from a servicing standpoint. We needed to make absolutely sure that the quality of service and level of personal recognition we provided to all our customers not only didn't diminish but improved."

American Express's management team had many alternatives other than pursuing the customer-adjacency strategy. It could have focused nearly all of the company's investment spending on international markets, which now account for 34 percent of the company's business. It could have migrated to a lending-based business, as many of American Express's bank card competitors did, or tried a different version of the earlier strategy, adding more financial services for core customers. It could have shifted resources to its investment-adviser business, making it the strategic focus.

For American Express, however, the right focus certainly turned out to be its redefinition of the business model, as Chenault describes, around a few core rules: focus on the brand, build flexibility into the business, and use the company's information assets to better understand customer preferences and design products and services specifically for them. Those formerly hidden assets—data, customer access, and trusted brand—have led to a new strategy to sell services based on the indications of that information. The one-size-fits-all approach became a relic of the past. The company expanded its product offering one hundredfold. Co-branded partnerships with major airlines, hotels, and retailers proliferated. Rewards programs using these insights from segmentation spurred record growth in cardmember spending and strengthened customer loyalty. Since that strategic shift, the company has averaged a return to shareholders of 20 percent per year.

Our case studies show repeatedly that hidden customer assets can provide a path to salvation when your strategy is approaching a limit. De Beers did it by shifting from a supply-centered strategy to a demand-centered strategy that was enabled by its unique access to and reputation among diamond dealers and their ultimate consumers. Autodesk did it by rediscovering untapped potential to drive deeper vertical segmentation in its original core customer base of architects and design engineers, shedding a broad-based services strategy in the process and going "back to the future." Hyperion Solutions did it by taking advantage of access to and credibility with its historical franchise with corporate finance directors to expand its suite of applications and gain share of wallet in those customers. And American Express did it by using a range of unexploited customer assets that it possessed, especially its unique database, derived from its direct relationships with both cardmembers and merchants.

But after you have noted your undervalued assets, how do you know what to do with them? Sometimes it is obvious. Occasionally, a brilliant bolt of lightning strikes. Or the nature of your business may allow management to test a range of paths in pilot projects, learning and studying further until the answer emerges. But what if those approaches don't work? Are there other places to look for ideas or guidance?

One place to look for insight is outside your four walls in parallel worlds. These could be other industries where dynamics similar to those your company faces have already played out, providing lessons as well as ideas. Or you might find the answers in your leading-edge customers who are using your products in new ways to solve their problems.

Finding Hidden Customer Assets

Suppose you are in a business that fits our criteria as a candidate for strategic renewal. The historic growth formula in your core customer base is not yielding the profit or growth it once did, as in the case of De Beers. Or the business model that was once unique has lost its power of differentiation, as with American Express. Or the profit pool is compressing, as it is for nearly all telecommunications companies, which are scrambling to find new ways to slice and dice their marketplaces and looking for differentiated assets (such as access to the home, ubiquity, or brand name) on which to rebuild.

How do you determine whether you have customer advantages that you can use to rejuvenate your strategy?

One method that proceeds from the inside-out consists of looking at the three types of customer assets—hidden segments, information, and privileged access (and their subcategories)—and asking your frontline managers whether they believe that such assets exist. If a logical case is put forward, attack it analytically to test whether it does exist, is differentiated, and can be exploited to redefine your business model. In some cases, such as American Express, this is what happened.

The other method operates *outside-in* and consists of looking at relevant success patterns outside your four walls.

Insights from Parallel Worlds

Where do you go for ideas about how to redefine your customer strategy in new and effective ways? We probed for the origin of these ideas in our case studies. We found that even though strategic insights emerged internally, just as often they were triggered by observing strategies of companies in other industries or lead user customers in a company's own industry. We call these *parallel worlds.*

The power of parallel worlds to generate insight and ideas is not new, but few companies believe that they are excellent at doing this. For instance, a Bain & Company study of business innovation found that only 28 percent of executives believed that their company was good at looking beyond its four walls for innovative ideas. Yet some of the most successful corporate rejuvenations of the past few years, such as Procter & Gamble's, have been fueled by a renewed emphasis on what we have termed *open-market innovation*, in which companies create deep partnerships with their customers, their suppliers and even companies outside their industry to develop new offerings and ideas.[11]

A recent study showed that it is usually better to be a well-funded fast follower than a first entrant into a new product market. The authors of that study state, "It is one of the great myths of business history that the first movers in a new market end up dominating the market. Nothing could be further from the truth when it comes to new-to-the-world markets that are created by radical innovation."[12] They cite a long list of examples, including CAT scanners (EMI developed them, but GE ended up being the strong leader and creator of the mass market); video games (Atari developed them, but Nintendo and later Sony reaped the benefits); and pocket calculators (Bowmar developed them, but Texas Instruments fully commercialized and took over the market).

Even for the simplest single core business, it is difficult for management teams to be as externally focused as perhaps they should be. It is even more difficult for complex, multicore businesses facing deep strategic issues.

Nearly all of our examples of successful change in the fundamentals of the customer model follow one or more basic patterns of business model evolution. The key is to conduct deep customer research and determine which model best fits your situation. You gain a twofold benefit by heeding the lessons from parallel worlds (single-customer observations, competitors with new approaches, and, most of all, success patterns in other industries). First, as shown in the list that follows, it's useful to have a checklist for thinking about how your business might need to change at the earliest stage of brainstorming and option development. Second, there can be great value in studying specific examples—disappointments as well as successes—from outside your company.

In our study, customer models evolved along one or more of the following seven dimensions.

- Products to services and information

- Commodity to differentiated (product)

- Homogeneous to segmented (customer)

- Components to systems

- Activities (disintegrated) to solutions (integrated)

- High to low cost (systems economics)

- Disconnected to networked

It is amazing how many times these customer models have played out in industry after industry, sometimes with success and sometimes with disaster. You can learn valuable lessons by going to school at the expense of others.

Brunswick: Creating a New Customer Model

Brunswick Corporation, the recreational products company, has experienced a rejuvenation through better operations as well as a more customer-centered strategy that draws on a series of observations of customer models outside the industry. To appreciate the transformation that has taken place—indeed, is still taking place—at Brunswick, you need some background. This company has followed a 158-year path from market pioneer to greatness to diversification and decay, and then back again to greatness.

John Brunswick wanted to build the best billiard table in the world and sell it throughout the United States, and in 1848 he started a company in Cincinnati to do just that. Like many companies with long histories, Brunswick focused on its core markets (billiards and bowling) for more than one hundred years. In 1956 Brunswick and its rival, AMF Company, pioneered the automatic pin setter in bowling alleys. That led to a resurgence of the game and a new, attractive profit pool.

Flush with its success, Brunswick's leaders at the time declared that they wanted the company to become the "General Motors of recreation," a mixed metaphor that triggered a wild streak of acquisitions. Brunswick jumped from the focus and expansion phases of the FER cycle into a frenzied attempt at redefinition. It bought companies that produced roller skates, outdoor clothes, fishing reels, golf clubs, baseballs, outboard motors, and boat hulls. It even moved into medical distribution and the manufacture of syringes.

Brunswick's company history doesn't explain the connection between these latter moves and recreation; it simply refers to the company during its feverish deal-making period as being "like a gambler on a hot streak." A few bets paid off, mostly those related to boating. But the other acquisitions caused a mass of confusion, destroyed millions of dollars in value, and sapped the company's energy and resources. One article on Brunswick refers to these two periods as "life number one and number two," as if the company were a cat.[13]

Life number three began when George Buckley joined the company's Mercury boat engine division and then rose to become CEO and chairman of Brunswick Corporation in 2000. By then, Brunswick's strategic misadventures had created a monumental challenge. Says Buckley:

> I knew in the first week what we had to do. We were $320 million into a $400 million line of credit. The stock price had dropped over three years from $37 to $12 per share. The corporation was headed to a loss-making year, and many businesses were losing large amounts of cash. We had nearly a year of inventory in some business units. There were huge write-offs, demoralized employees, angry shareholders . . . and a potential liquidity crisis. A nice way to start! When you are in the middle of the Atlantic Ocean with a hole in the bottom of your boat, the only thing you need to know how to do right then is bail. I knew we had to get cash into the company, that I was on the hot seat, and that we needed to create urgency around a plan.[14]

In the next two years, the company cut costs extensively, closed multiple plants, and exited businesses from fishing equipment to coolers to camping. That stabilized things. But what next? That's where Buckley's parallel-world idea came in:

> A technique I have used throughout my career is the parallel worlds approach. The Bible says there is nothing new under the sun. In physics, the same mathematical equations describe the penetration of water through a dam wall, heat through steel blocks, and eddy currents in magnetic materials. If I have a difficult problem, I always ask myself if someone else has solved it before in another situation.

We realized . . . that the same evolution of product performance and reliability needed in the boat business had occurred years before in the automotive business and that there were strong parallels we could learn from. It is about going to the consumer to see what they needed, and then working backwards to see what was needed by the distributor (or dealer) and then see what changes this implied in our own economics and manufacturing model. I created what I called some "imagine" slides and said, "Imagine if there were only one Toyota that had global presence, great after-market service, low costs, and broad product lines, served all markets, and had dealers who were made rich and passionate by the quality of the products this company sold. And then imagine what would happen if all other manufacturers made cars like they did in 1970. Progressively, share would migrate to this company, competitors would respect you, and investors and customers would love you. But here is the parallel: in boating, this company can be Brunswick. If we execute this list of actions with products and services, we will become like this symbolic car company. We want to become the Toyota of marine.

The analogy with the evolution of the automobile industry has provided Brunswick with some of the key elements of a strategy road map. Buckley explains:

We realized that we had a huge advantage to pulling this off because we made engines as well as boats, which no one else in our business does. So we have the chance to create the fully integrated "end-to-end" boat, just as the auto business [in its earlier years] moved from products that resemble kit cars with lots of after-market components to sales of superbly engineered, completely integrated cars. Integration is the key here, because I have noticed in life that things go wrong mostly at the boundaries. Eliminate the interfaces and boundaries and you will improve product reliability. So that was our concept for boats; cut the component boundaries out and go for a fully integrated product. If we could get control end-to-end, we could satisfy customer needs better. Would you ever buy a car whose dash was equipped with a red-colored square bezel speedometer and round grey-colored engine-revolution counter? I don't think so. Yet that is what we did in boating. When I was a boy and my father owned a British car, we maintained it every Sunday afternoon. (You had to in those days.) Even turn signals were often after-market components you had to add! Now it is all integrated . . . I realized that the same is happening in boats, yet we are at a much earlier stage in the cycle.

Brunswick has acquired Navman and Northstar Technologies, thus bringing it technologies in GPS navigation, marine electronics, and systems integration. This segment of the business grew at 105 percent per year between 2002 and 2005, and in 2005 was closing in on $400 million in revenue. Brunswick also acquired Land 'N' Sea, the industry's largest North American distributor of parts, which offers same-day service and delivery on critical boat parts. Recently, Brunswick revised its organizational structure to bring these strategies of customer and product integration into markets outside North America.

Brunswick bottomed out in 2001 with revenues of $3.3 billion. By 2005 it had grown to $5.9 billion, with operating earnings of $479 million. The stock price rose from a low of $13.71 in 2001 to a high of $48.91 in November 2004. This is a company with a new core: some 91 percent of revenues and profits come from the marine business; the original billiard and bowling core accounts for most of the rest. Brunswick has a leading 38 percent U.S. market share of outboard motors. It is significantly larger than Yamaha, which, with $1.5 billion in comparable products, is its nearest similar competitor.

George Buckley concludes:

> For my guidance I looked to all sorts of places. George Bernard Shaw said the reasonable man adapts himself to the system, the unreasonable man adapts the system to himself. There are times when you have to be unreasonable. It is possible to be unreasonable in an encouraging way through a vision that is realizable and may even have parallels in other industries or other worlds that you can observe. It often starts as one person's dream, but it cannot remain that way. Faith is a non–knowledge-based system, but trust is an experience-based system. It starts with faith and becomes trust. If you can engage the organization in realizing the dream and translating it to their dream, then it is in all people's dreams. Even if the vision evolves, as it often does, these principles still apply. And that is incredibly powerful.

It is difficult to transform the basic customer model, and most attempts end in disappointment. But Brunswick had no choice except to do it right or go under. It focused on the customers it had in its only sustainable core, boating, and created a business that redefined the company's relationship to those customers. Instead of offering them parts—a boat, an engine, an accessory—it began offering them an integrated system, complete with after-sale parts.

Identifying Hidden Customer Assets

This chapter has proposed the idea that the complexity of your business may mask pockets of leadership economics: in a customer segment, in the solution to a specific type of customer problem, or through unique information and access.

If you see yourself in the types of situations described here, ask yourself the following questions. If you see dilemmas in the answers, it's probable that the search for undervalued segments and unexploited customer access might prove to be fruitful.

Identifying Hidden Customer Assets

Do you have hidden customer assets that could form the basis of your renewal strategy or at least fuel a wave of profitable growth? The answers to these questions can help you decide:

- Who are your core customers, really? How is that changing?

- Where are you truly differentiated to those core customers? How do you know?

- In which customer segments are you the leader? Why? Have you fully exploited that lead?

- Do you possess a database or repository of knowledge about your customers' behaviors or economics? Is it critical and unique data? Have you probed its full potential?

- Do you have unexploited levels of influence—brand, trust, or access—to some of those segments? How do you know?

- Have you examined the right parallel worlds (see the section "Insights from Parallel Worlds") for ideas on the next general version of your business model?

- Where are the profit pools now and in the future of your core customer base? Are you well positioned with regard to where they're shifting?

Underutilized Capabilities

Capabilities are the elements of business. If there were a business equivalent of Mendeleev's periodic table of the elements (which describes the building blocks of all matter in the known universe), capabilities would populate the cells of that table. Given energy and time, you can combine capabilities to create new properties and powers. Like inert elements, some capabilities are irrelevant to each other, but others can be combined in surprising ways. Such combinations can have multiplier effects and create enormous commercial power for change or renewal.

Capabilities are the third, and the most hidden, of the underexploited assets in our study. Tapping in to them is critical to the strategic renewal of many businesses, as well as for strategic incursions on less capable rivals. In the following examples, differences among a handful of competitors in a few key capabilities render the trajectory of the losers unsustainable, while the winner seems almost unstoppable.

U.K. grocery chains Tesco and Sainsbury's were once nearly identical. Today, Tesco is the clear winner, with 31 percent market share and a superior economic model, and Sainsbury's has dropped to number 3 in the marketplace behind Wal-Mart-owned ASDA. The key factor? Capabilities. Early in the game, Tesco recognized the competitive importance of superior logistics and replenishment. As a result, Tesco began to outinvest its competitors by a wide margin.

Looking back on this remarkable case of competitive separation, Lord Ian MacLaurin, CEO at Tesco during much of the period, said, "We focused first on distribution capabilities. We eventually became so good that we could run smaller stores efficiently, where others could not, such as Tesco Metro and Tesco Express formats. In addition, we felt we had a superior level in-stock of key items in our large stores. Through it all, distribution was the thing; many of our competitors still have not gotten their distribution capabilities right even after all of this time."[1]

Or consider the case of package delivery. The capability battle between UPS, FedEx, and the U.S. Postal Service for control over premium letter and parcel delivery is an uneven battle. USPS is constrained in its ability to hire, pay, compete, and invest by legislation governing it as a public entity. By contrast, UPS and FedEx have invested aggressively in sophisticated capabilities in package tracking and IT systems for advanced logistics, spending on average about 8 percent of sales over the past five years. As a result, UPS and FedEx have grown from less than one-quarter the size of USPS in the 1980s to (combined) nearly the same size as the postal service and are still growing 50 percent faster.

Many factors come into play; some might argue that USPS can use earnings from its monopoly in letter delivery to subsidize its competition in parcels. But if you talk to people on both sides of this battle, you find that a central element is the growing capability gap that affects the cost of delivery, the speed and frequency of delivery and special features (such as package tracking software). The capability gap with private carriers, and the reinvestment levels required to compete, is one reason many postal services in Europe, such as Deutsche Post and TNT, have been privatized. These governments have decided to exit a capability battle that was redefining their competitors faster than themselves.

In the market of Internet searches, Google entered the fray in 1998, behind a range of competitors such as Yahoo!, Excite, and Ask Jeeves (now known as Ask.com). Today, Google has about

50 percent market share and has expanded from this strong core into a range of related business opportunities. The company now has $6 billion in revenues and a market value of $153 billion, or 77 percent of the value of Wal-Mart, the number 1 company on the *Fortune* 500 list.

Central to Google's success are its software design capabilities and the proprietary page-sorting algorithm at its core. Google apparently has recognized that its competitive strength hinges on the search position, Google's unique ecosystem of users and suppliers (for example, it has more than three hundred thousand advertising partners in AdWords), and the capability of its software designers. Google has intensified the quest for this talent to a new level that has shocked the industry, mirroring the free agent mania that we see in the salaries of sports figures. For instance, Google hired away Microsoft's leading speech-recognition software expert with a pay package reported to be valued at about $10 million. This shouldn't surprise us; a company that realizes it is ultimately competing on capabilities is willing to invest heavily in them.

In our Capability Survey of global executives, 57 percent of respondents said it was "extremely important" to acquire a new core capability in order to reach their growth targets (an amazing 98 percent said it was either important or extremely important). When we asked them to list any "hidden gems already in the business that could fuel growth," the two most frequent responses were forms of unexploited capabilities.

In a separate Bain & Company analysis of more than one hundred strategy studies for clients, project leaders indicated that in 56 percent of the cases the new strategy that had been developed hinged on unexploited and underappreciated capabilities—either on their own or in combination with other capabilities that needed to be acquired or strengthened. In more than half the cases, the missing or inadequate capability was one that would improve a cost position; in another 45 percent it was a capability that was central to speed or product cycle time. These are fundamental needs and dimensions that typically are at the heart of differences in competitive performance.

What Is a Capability?

A capability, as referred to here, is the ability to get something done, to accomplish a highly specific task, in a repeatable fashion. Capabilities are the building blocks of the value chains of business. The typical business unit comprises eighty to two hundred significant capabilities, of which a much smaller number are truly core. We define a core capability by its ability to create economic value (for a customer) and by its ability to provide a source of differentiation against competitors. This is not to say that other capabilities are not important—such as sending bills to customers, managing the company's intranet, or training employees—but these usually are not core. Nor are they the types of hidden assets that one can use to renew a business strategy.

The concept of "core competence" is familiar in the business lexicon, as is its corollary: that businesses are built on a basic set of capabilities that shapes their ability to compete. The seminal article on the subject, published in 1990, was "The Core Competence of the Corporation," by Gary Hamel and C. K. Prahalad. Commenting later in their book *Competing for the Future,* the authors said this:

> There is nothing very novel in the proposition that firms compete on capability. The subtlety comes when one attempts to distinguish between those competencies or capabilities that are "core" and those that are "non core." If one produced an inventory of all the capabilities that are potentially important to success in a particular business, it would be a long list indeed—too long to be of any great managerial usefulness. Senior management can't pay equal attention to everything; there must be some sense of what activities really contribute to long-term corporate prosperity. The goal, therefore, is to focus senior management's attention on those competencies that lie at the center, rather than the periphery, of long-term competitive success.[2]

In 1996, Michael Porter wrote that seldom could lasting competitive advantage be attained simply by superior operational effectiveness, and that to be a success, it was necessary to perform different activities and not just similar activities in somewhat better ways.[3] He described this strategy through what he called "activity systems": the ways that a company's capabilities link to others to create business processes, and the ways that those processes can multiply the power of one another and create competitive advantage that can be hard to replicate. Porter cited the example of IKEA, a highly successful Swedish furniture retailer. He showed how IKEA's unique business formula could be traced to a strong set of linked capabilities (design for assembly, logistics, and cost management) in ways that were unique in the industry.

It is easier to determine how hidden capabilities might help you reshape your strategy if you divide them into four types:

- Capabilities that are core to you because they are highly differentiated and are essential if you are to create customer value.

- Capabilities that are not differentiated (they are similar for all players in your industry) but are essential to create value. These undifferentiated but critical capabilities give you opportunities to innovate in the quest for new competitive differentiation. Often, it is exactly in these key undifferentiated capabilities that new competitors find their formula for market entry.

- Capabilities that do not drive very much economic value and are not differentiated (pure commodities, which often are candidates for outsourcing).

- Capabilities that create limited value but that you need to do uniquely.

Layered on top of this static framework are the capabilities you need for the future. What will the picture look like in five years? What should it look like? Where and when can you obtain the required new capabilities? Where do you need to strengthen weak capabilities? Which strong core capabilities should you invest in and extend in new ways? How do the new and old capabilities interact to create something new?

Many new patterns and strategic possibilities can emerge in surprising ways from a focused discussion of capabilities. My observation is that few management teams have had such a conversation ("What are our three or four most differentiating capabilities today, and how will that need to change in five years?").

This chapter examines the ways that capabilities emerge as the determining factor in companies that have redefined their strategies successfully, and in companies that were not able to pull it off. This factor is slightly different from hidden customer assets and hidden platform assets. In those cases, the key is the uniqueness of assets you already possess and their potential role in creating clear and immediate competitive differentiations. (For instance, PerkinElmer's genetic sequencing products and patents—buried in the company— were unique to it. Marvel's ownership of Spider-Man was unavailable to others. Dometic's strong leadership in certain segments of refrigeration might have been coveted by others but was uncontested.) Capabilities are different from the other kinds of hidden assets because, in theory, capabilities are often available to others. Another key is that their impact on the organization and on ultimate competitive advantage often resides in the complex chemistry by which new capabilities can alter the potential of everything around them, creating something distinctly new and better: a higher synthesis (as the examples in this chapter will make clear).

Thus, not only is it more difficult to directly observe capabilities than to observe businesses, orphan products, or customer databases, but also the impact of capabilities is more subtle. This is why we deem them to be the most hidden assets of all.

Three Patterns of Underutilized Capabilities

This chapter presents our discoveries about hidden capabilities and explains how to recognize them and how to think about their latent potential to redefine a core business and its strategy. It examines three situations that we found in our research:

- Capabilities can be found at the corporate level, with their impact rippling downward through the businesses and product lines.

- Capabilities can allow a management team to restructure the economic model of a particular business and redefine what it can deliver to its core customers.

- Capabilities can act as catalysts in the creation of an entirely new core, one that perhaps has the potential to become more valuable than the previous core.

Redefinition Through Hidden Capabilities: Companywide Change

The capability that proves to drive transformation in a company may exist at the corporate level—at the center—and can be used to reshape a range of businesses and product lines. We begin with the case of Novozymes, the global leader in the production of enzymes. This example is somewhat ironic, because enzymes interact with other elements in their surroundings to enable new levels of performance, a metaphor for what capabilities can do in a business.

Novozymes: Capabilities as Catalysts to Redefinition. Enzymes are naturally occurring proteins that trigger and accelerate chemical reactions. In fact, the word *enzyme* is Greek for "in yeast," the leavening effect of yeast being one of the earliest recognized enzymatic reactions. Environmentally friendly, effective, and organic in their structure, enzymes are gradually taking over many commercial tasks from traditional chemicals. Enzymes can decompose milk protein to make cheese and yogurt, speed up the process of brewing beer, improve the ability of detergents to remove stains, accelerate the process of converting grain to ethanol, and slow down the natural process by which bread turns stale.

Novozymes has grown to become the world leader in the development and production of high-quality enzymes. In 2004, Novozymes reached DKK6 billion in revenues, with 18 percent profit margins. It held an average 44 percent share across its markets, many of which the company had created from whole cloth.

As with many of the companies in this book, Novozymes' ancestry goes back many years. Two competitors—Nordisk and Novo—were founded in the early 1920s to extract insulin from pork glands. In 1940, Novo realized that the spent glands contained an enzyme called tripsin that could be used in making digestive aids and in tanning leather. During World War II Novo was called upon to produce penicillin, so it added capabilities in fermentation and high-volume production. After the war, the company focused on high-volume commodity enzymes, initially for applications in washing powders and then in brewing. These early applications were not high science; in fact, the brewing enzyme was based on a two-thousand-year-old technique developed in Japan to accelerate rice fermentation in the production of sake.

In 1988, Novo and Nordisk combined to form Novo Nordisk and in 2000, the organization spun off Novozymes in a public offering as a separate company focused on enzymes. The CEO of the new company was Steen Riisgaard, a twenty-one-year industry veteran who was president of Novo Nordisk at the time of the spin-off. Riisgaard began to move Novozymes away from its dependence on commodity enzymes. The company obtained leading-edge biochemical capabilities, which made it possible to produce designer enzymes for specific applications. Novozymes' scientists were increasingly driven to work closely with customers rather than pursue research in isolation. Riisgaard explains the importance of these capabilities:

> Only the closest possible technical relationships with the most technically competent customers drive real breakthroughs. This is a major capability we have worked at over the years. In fact, today, we do not allow any exploratory research for more than six months without such on-site customer verification. This is a real difference from the business of the past.

We have created our competitive advantage through the successive waves of capabilities we have added and integrated into our core. Each has changed what we can do with customers significantly and had impacts that we could not have predicted. The first big scientific capability was the introduction of genetic engineering. Until nearly 1990 we found most of our enzymes in nature . . . Now we can engineer improvements directly in the laboratory through mutations and design enzymes to customer specifications . . . The next major capability was protein engineering . . . followed by building capabilities in artificial evolution and "gene shuffling" emerging from the sequencing technologies used for the human genome.[4]

Suppose a customer wants a way to remove grease stains from laundry at unusually low temperatures. Novozymes would collect possible enzyme-producing microorganisms from ecological hot spots all over the world. Researchers using advanced robots would examine the functions of these organisms to find the one that produced an enzyme closest to what was needed. Then they would take the microorganism into the laboratory, remove the relevant gene, insert the gene into a microorganism that can safely be produced in high volume, and offer the new product to the customer. Riisgaard refers to this business as "finding a needle in a haystack"—except that Novozymes uses state-of-the-art technologies both to single out the haystack and to speed the process of finding the needle.

Such capabilities have not only distinguished Novozymes from its competitors but have also shortened product-development times, a huge advantage. The current benchmark for development of a new technical enzyme—including discovery, development, approval, toxicological experiments, filing, and commercialization—is twenty-four months. It used to be five years.

From an average position in one product, Novozymes has developed commanding market shares in a wide range of segments. It has transformed itself from a business selling a couple of known, lower-margin commodity products into a company that can design enzymes for a wide range of tailored applications, creating new, higher-margin micromarkets in the process. The new capabilities propelled the change.

Novozymes has built capabilities at the company level to enhance, differentiate, and spawn enzyme-related businesses. Sometimes you can take capabilities at the company level, spanning several businesses, a step further, as an integrated management system that can be applied to a range of businesses to create unique economic value. Such a system is the Holy Grail of corporations as well as private equity firms, and one that few find. But some do. One that distinguished itself in the way it collected and shaped such bundles of capabilities is Danaher.

Danaher: Discovering Repeatability in Improving Performance. In 1987 Danaher Corporation was an industrial company with $617 million in revenues. Almost all its business was concentrated in industrial tools. Today, the company is transformed. From 1987 through 2005, revenues grew at 16 percent per year to $7.9 billion. Increases in margins helped push net income to $898 million, and the stock price rose more than 5,000 percent, outperforming the stock market by more than five times. Danaher has accomplished this transformation not by focusing on a single core but by creating a formula that has allowed it to expand to six strategic platforms and 102 subunits within these platforms. The platforms span a wide range of industrial applications, from electronic testing to environmental services.

The force behind Danaher's transformation was a repeatable model for identifying acquisitions, executing them, and adding value. Our work on frequent acquirers shows that companies that make many small and medium-sized acquisitions have by far the highest success record. From 1987 through 1995, Danaher made 1.5 acquisitions per year averaging about $80 million; since that time, the company has made acquisitions at a rate of more than 6 per year, averaging $100 million.

It has focused on five main criteria: niche businesses, leadership positions in the core, consistency with identified strategic platforms, medium size, and purchase prices that allow room to earn returns. At acquisition, every company is immediately put under something called the Danaher Business System, a central pillar in the growth strategy that management articulates to analysts. This system is critical for a company in which acquisitions have driven more than 50 percent of the growth during this period of extraordinary stock performance.

The Danaher Business System has several phases and dimensions, including productivity improvement, sourcing techniques, measurement, control, and values. So far, it has proven repeatable, has consistently built value, and has become the envy of many other companies that aspire to transform themselves through acquisition of new cores.

Yet few companies have achieved this level of performance, and even fewer by honing their capabilities for adding and managing a series of semirelated cores. Danaher is one of the few major corporations that has managed to pull off what many aspire to accomplish. Others that have done it during their growth periods include Emerson Electric, Valspar (industrial coatings), Medtronic (implantable devices), and Johnson & Johnson. Companies that aspired to have a repeatable formula or vision for diversification include Kvaerner, Marconi, Vivendi, W. R. Grace, and the granddaddy of all conglomerates, Harold Geneen's ITT Industries.

The bottom line? Beware. If you think you have a repeatable corporate capability to improve businesses that you buy, don't be so sure. This kind of strategy has been powerful for a few but a siren's song for many. Prove to yourself that it really adds value differentially, and understand how that is possible when everyone is trying to do the same thing and few are finding success.

P&G: Rejuvenation Through Customer Capabilities. Procter & Gamble, under CEO A. G. Lafley, has accomplished an impressive revival by tapping in to underused capabilities found deep in the bones of the company. These are the skills, pioneered in many areas of consumer products by P&G, of analyzing consumer behavior for unique insights that shape product development. It has worked. Since

Lafley's takeover in 2000, P&G's stock price (up nearly 125 percent) has outgrown the S&P index by nearly a factor of three. The company, which watched its operating income dip in the period 1998 to 2001 from $6 billion to $4.7 billion, has seen it rebound to $13.2 billion in 2006. This is impressive for a one-hundred-seventy-year-old company in a set of markets whose average growth rate mirrors the 3 percent (or so) annual growth of the U.S. GDP.

For example, consider the renewal of P&G's oral-care category and how it changed a declining, nonleadership business position. Michael Kehoe, former president of the dental products business, commented on the rejuvenation of the Crest product line, which went from losing market share (to Colgate) to high-double-digit growth. The strategy was built on multiple brands and a consumer-focused (versus product-focused) approach to the market:

> We had become too narrow and internally focused in our view of the market and our consumers. Competitors were redefining the entire category, pushing into cosmetic and aesthetic benefits like whitening and breath, new health-based toothpastes, peroxide products, and so on, and they were growing much faster than Crest as a result. We hit the low point at the end of the 1990s. The key in our renewal was becoming much more consumer focused through a series of specific approaches and tools, as well as broadening the definition of what our brand stood for, allowing us to innovate around a whole new set of consumer needs. Now we see consumer trends and behaviors as the heart of our strategy as opposed to products. We believe we have become the best at methods for consumer learning and, thus, are best informed on strategy for toothpastes, rinses, whitening products— whatever the consumer chooses to get the benefits they want—and then focusing on getting them to market first. This is a competitive advantage that comes from building up those capabilities.[5]

Companywide capabilities can come in many forms, and it is often difficult to detect and prove them. But when they occur, they can be powerful forces for redefinition. The three examples you've seen show the various ways that this can occur. Novozymes developed superior capabilities to bring in new science and commercialize it in all its business platforms. Danaher discovered that it had the elements of a management system that it could refine, codify, and apply to companies having a specific predictive profile, companies it then acquired and improved. P&G, in a sense, rediscovered and rejuvenated its core capability to understand customers deeply, a capability that was once the hallmark of the company. These abilities became a linchpin for renewal of some of the business units, including the dental products business, based on a new, more customer-centered strategy.

We turn now to the second of three ways that previously unexploited capabilities played an important role in the metamorphosis of a business whose growth path was slowing down.

Redefinition Through Hidden Capabilities: Changing the Business Model

The discovery of unexploited capabilities, in combination with new capabilities, can change what you deliver to customers and how you do it.

Boston Scientific: A Chain Reaction of Capabilities. Less invasive surgery (LIS) has been a mantra in parts of the medical community for more than a decade as medical technology has advanced. The breakthrough product for many of these procedures was the steerable catheter, and eventually the balloon catheter. This is a long plastic tube containing somewhat rigid guide wires inside, and sometimes a tip, such as a small inflatable balloon. Catheters can be introduced into the body with a small incision and then used to open a clogged vessel.

Such steerable catheters were the first product made by Boston Scientific (BSC), which was founded in Massachusetts in 1979 by

John Abele and Peter Nicholas. Since then, the company has been in the forefront of many premier products in one of the hottest medical markets for decades. Over time, the company extended the use of its steerable catheter into heart, vascular, respiratory, urological, and other internal applications. Through these developments and a series of acquisitions, Boston Scientific had expanded by 1997 to about $1.9 billion in revenues, with its market capitalization reaching more than $12 billion midyear.

But there were storm clouds on the horizon. In 1998, the company experienced a costly product recall, was beset by an accounting controversy, and missed its profit targets for the second year in a row. After a couple of years of turbulence, the company's market value would plunge by more than 50 percent by end of 2000.

However, a new CEO, Jim Tobin, had entered the company in 1999 after a successful run as CEO at Biogen and a long career as one of the most respected executives at Baxter International. Tobin and his team quickly began to understand the situation they faced. The company needed what Tobin refers to as a "new playbook." The capabilities that had propelled the company in the past—product focus, the ability to choose and execute on small, related acquisitions, and its deep knowledge of LIS—were no longer sufficient in a more complex and more competitive world.

Specifically, the company faced three growing, somewhat hidden liabilities. First, BSC was subscale relative to emerging competitors such as Johnson & Johnson. Second, BSC was high cost in manufacturing and operations; the tremendous product flow of the preceding decade had created high-margin products, with limited pressure to lower costs. As a result, modern manufacturing best practices did not exist, an increasing liability in a difficult marketplace. Third, BSC's financial profile did not support an R&D effort to match its competitors'. What to do?

Since 2000, Boston Scientific has implemented three waves of strategic initiatives, each building on the preceding initiative, and each larger and bolder than the last. The first wave combined operational restructuring with a drive to manufacturing excellence (and a reinvestment in R&D). The second phase involved development and successful launch of the drug-eluting stent, a short tube of wire and drug-impregnated plastic that improved the performance of stents in heart surgery. The third, and current, phase was the acquisition of Guidant, one of the leaders in cardiac rhythm management and a participant in Boston Scientific's core interventional cardiology business.

In one of the largest medical acquisitions ever completed, in 2006 Boston Scientific purchased Guidant for $27 billion after a bidding war with J&J. In the process, a smaller player whose growth seemed to stall out at $2.6 billion in revenues in 2000 (a 6% decline from the previous year) has leapfrogged into position as the leading company in the world in its core markets of cardiac and vascular surgery and interventional cardiology.

What started this chain reaction? As in any complex story, there were many factors. However, when I traced the chain back to the first link, through discussions with executives who were there at the time, I found at least one root cause: Tobin and his team prioritized and succeeded at integrating production facilities and bringing world-class manufacturing and process-flow capabilities into the company. The impact was fast and impressive. Despite a highly competitive environment, the gross profit percentage (revenues above factory cost and labor) increased from 65 percent to 69 percent. Boston Scientific invested the entire improvement in R&D, increasing it from 9 percent of revenues to 12 percent of revenues and driving R&D spending from $200 million in 1998 to $343 million in 2002. In addition, the management team narrowed and intensified that spending on fewer priorities, particularly new generations of cardiovascular stents.

The R&D spending proved to be effective, especially combined with a hidden asset discovered out of the blue. With the acquisition of Schneider Worldwide, a company purchased in 1998, Boston Scientific obtained the rights for medical device use of a styrene-based plastic material called SIBS. BSC's testing proved that this material satisfied the requirements for the next generation of stents.

In that next wave of products, drugs that prevented the gradual growth of scar tissue were infused in the walls of the stent. (When scar tissue forms blockages, the stent can shut down, requiring risky and undesirable reoperation. The drug-eluting stents reduced the probability of this narrowing—called restenosis—significantly.) The narrow set of requirements included nonreactivity with the human body as well as durability, flexibility, the ability to hold drugs in its structure, and most important, the ability to release those drugs steadily and slowly. This was a key ingredient of the Taxus stent launched by Boston Scientific in the U.S. market in March 2004. The product was such a success that it became the market leader in two months, with 70 percent market share.

But it was the operating capabilities in manufacturing that Tobin and his team brought to BSC that liberated resources in R&D to develop the new stent and to discover the properties of the hidden asset they had received from Schneider (which, at the time of the acquisition, had been written down to zero, as having no clear use).

Some observers have referred to Taxus as the most successful new medical product launch in history. It generated $1.4 billion in sales in its first four months. By early 2006, Taxus accounted for 60% of BSC's operating profits, and had helped increase revenues from $3.5 billion to $6.3 billion and driven the company's market value through the roof.

The next act of Boston Scientific's strategy is unfolding only now. The acquisition of Guidant has sparked both praise and controversy; initially it was widely lauded, but not long afterward, it came under fire when BSC suffered some setbacks, brought on by recalls of Guidant cardiac devices and concerns about drug-coated stents' link to a higher incidence of blood clots. Still, the acquisition made BSC the second-largest medical device company in the world, with leading positions in a range of products in some of the fastest-growing medical markets, including surgical stents and products for cardiac rhythm management. How this large, transforming acquisition will play out economically is a drama in its infancy waiting to unfold. However, it too was enabled by the capability-driven stent strategy described here.

Boston Scientific shows how an injection of world-class capabilities from 2000 through 2002 triggered a chain reaction, strengthening and liberating resources in the core business, driving a major new growth initiative (Taxus), and enabling the acquisition of Guidant. These moves resulted in a radically different company with much greater potential.

Transformation Through Hidden Capabilities: Creating a New Core

We have found that the revival of a company can come from spawning new core businesses from existing capabilities that prove to be extendable in new areas (in combination with newly acquired capabilities). This was true in the successive waves of change experienced in the transformation of Li & Fung from its origins as a trading company to the leader in logistics management in Asia. It also was true in the way PerkinElmer built its new life-sciences core from a dispersed set of products and capabilities. It was true in the case of Apple Computer, one of the most widely followed current stories of business revival. It was true in the case of De Beers's business unit, Element Six, which was formed to exploit a leading capability in synthetic industrial diamonds that has been built up for more than five decades.

Apple's ongoing revival, built on the success of iPod and on iTunes (its site for downloading music and videos), is an example of how a new cocktail of capabilities can create a new, potentially transformational core for a company.

A New Core for Apple. Apple has been universally admired, even idealized, by consumers for its brilliant products, but its financial success over the years has been mixed. From 1995 through 2005, the global market share of Apple Computers declined from 9 percent to less than 3 percent. Although the iPod music player was launched in 2001, Apple's stock had languished for fifteen years, leaving the company in 2003 with the same market value that it had had in 1987. From 1993 to 2003, the growth period of the personal computer, Apple's total return to shareholders was only 4 percent, and its return on equity at the end of the period was 2 percent despite a string of attempts at innovative product forays (the purchase of NeXT workstation systems, the Newton pen-driven PDA device, and so on).

Yet starting in 2003 with the launch of the iTunes Music Store, iPod sales took off. By June 2005, Apple had attained 70 percent of the market for portable MP3 players, up from 12 percent in the first quarter of 2003. In less than two years, the iTunes Music Store has captured 85 percent of the market for music downloads, which is expected to grow at an annual rate of 60 percent through 2008. Apple's market value exploded from $7 billion in June 2003 to $55 billion in March 2006.

The music business now accounts for nearly 50 percent of the company's total revenues, and 40 percent of profits. Though by no means complete, it has the potential to redefine Apple despite the lurking presence of many tough competitors, from Microsoft to the makers of cellular phones. Close observers of Apple's core strengths—design, brand management, the consumer user interface, and elegant, easy-to-use software—will recognize its historic core abilities coming together again, as in many other products, in the iPod and its subsequent versions.

What was a new capability, and a catalyst to the transformation, was Apple's preemptive ability to gain access to content by developing the iTunes Music Store, being the first to sign up the top four music-recording companies for paid, legal Internet downloads. Apple also created a brilliantly functional approach to digital rights management through its Fairplay software, whereby music purchased on iTunes will play only on the iPod platform; at the same time, music companies obtain a highly controllable royalty stream, accounting for 80 percent of the iTunes revenues. The symbiosis between iTunes and iPod has caused both products to take off and has created a unique barrier to entry. As iPods proliferate (more than thirty-nine million have been sold in 2006) and as iTunes downloads grow (at a rate of one million per day), the cost of switching from one system to another increases, making consumers reluctant to change players or use multiple download services.

In a report on the revitalization of Apple, J.P. Morgan reports as follows:

> The model did not really take off until Apple began to bundle the iTunes Music Store with the iPod. Indeed, Apple's iPod shipments were less than spectacular prior to the launch of the Music Store, averaging 113,000 units per quarter. In the December quarter, following the launch, however, Apple shipped 733,000 units, or 235 percent more than the previous year . . . Apple has created a solution that is in great demand, while larger companies with much larger R&D budgets are struggling to cobble together partnerships in order to keep up.[6]

So far, the iPod-based music strategy has been transformational for Apple. It is an example of a strategy to move away from a core—computers—that offered insufficient growth potential and toward a new profit pool. Early MP3 players were complex and frustrating to use. Apple not only improved the software but also created the easy-to-use online download platform iTunes, and, most important, organized the consumer product experience uniquely. If your iPod breaks, you can go online and arrange for Apple to send a shipping box with foam and labels in which to return the iPod. When you receive a new iPod, you simply attach it to the computer. In a few clicks, iTunes has restored your previous content and settings.

To accomplish this feat, though, Apple had to obtain new capabilities in digital rights management and music. Virtually all the value created by Apple in the past ten years can be attributed to hidden or underexploited assets and critical new capabilities that it acquired (figure 5-1).

FIGURE 5-1

Apple acquired and built significant new capabilities . . .

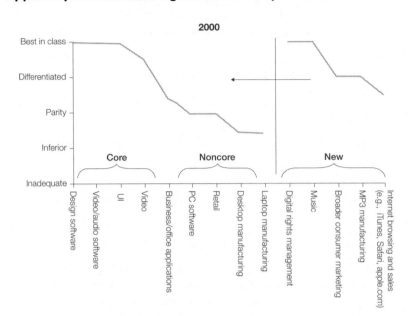

. . . and many of them formed the basis of the company's new core

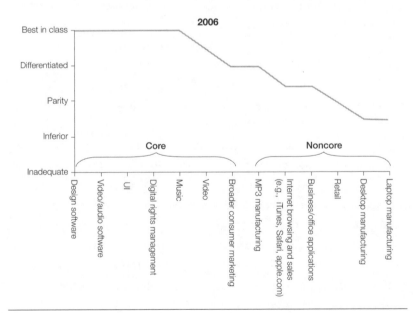

Assessing Your Own Capabilities

Most companies do not keep track of their capabilities as they do their businesses, product lines, departments, or even real estate. Ask your management team to list on a piece of paper the three or four capabilities that are most central to your ability to differentiate yourself against competitors or that create the most value for customers. Ask them how the situation will shift in the future. You might be surprised by the range—or the hesitancy—of their answers.

In my experience, few management teams can offer a crisp, consistent, and convincing list of capabilities in answer to these questions. Fewer still can point to clear external benchmarks of performance to prove differentiation, or to clear measures of the profit pool at each stage of the value chain to demonstrate where value is created by those capabilities. Why not? Perhaps it is tougher to see, feel, and touch capabilities than a customer database, a business unit, or a product line. Or perhaps in complex organizations, no one is responsible for a capability that cuts across organizational units (as many capabilities do). But you cannot manage something that you never measure or define. How ironic it is that the most elemental building blocks of competitive advantage— and the catalysts for changing strategic direction—are seldom well understood.

Four Useful Tools

This section describes four simple tools that can help you organize your thoughts and assemble data on capabilities as you develop your strategic options. These tools are depicted in figure 5-2.

A good starting point is the value chain (figure 5-2a), which shows each of the major activities (or clusters of activities) that the business employs to deliver value to customers. Figure 5-3, an expanded version of a typical value chain, shows the twenty primary categories of activities that we find.

FIGURE 5-2

Defining core capabilities: basic approach

a. What are the capabilities?

Value Chain

Design 〉 Sales 〉 Marketing 〉 Mfg. 〉 Logistics 〉 Service

Capabilities:

• Capability 1	• Capability 1	• Capability 1	• Capability 1	• Capability 1	• Capability 1
• Capability 2	• Capability 2	• Capability 2	• Capability 2	• Capability 2	• Capability 2
• Capability 3	• Capability 3	• Capability 3	• Capability 3	• Capability 3	• Capability 3
• ...	• ...	• ...	• ...	• ...	• ...

b. Which are core versus noncore?

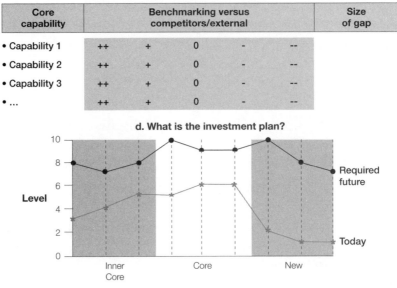

Inner core

Role in value creation

Noncore

Core

Non-essential

Degree of Differentiation

c. How do they compare versus competitors?

Core capability	Benchmarking versus competitors/external					Size of gap
• Capability 1	++	+	0	-	--	
• Capability 2	++	+	0	-	--	
• Capability 3	++	+	0	-	--	
• ...	++	+	0	-	--	

d. What is the investment plan?

Level

10 — 8 — 6 — 4 — 2 — 0

Required future

Today

Inner Core

Core

New

FIGURE 5-3

The value chain can be used to group capabilities

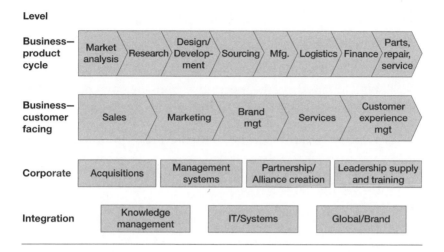

The point is not to catalog every single capability. That would add to the confusion. Rather, the value comes from identifying your core processes and activities, describing as rigorously as possible where you are (or are not) advantaged, and understanding how that is driven by a subset of capabilities—the crown jewels of competitive advantage.

The four tools in figure 5-2 are simple in conception but can be difficult to develop, agree upon, or demonstrate with data. Yet the outcome of this exercise in preparation for revising your strategy can prove to be fundamental to the answer. As mentioned, the value chain is a good starting place to visualize your company's key activities, the capabilities that underlie them, and the data in which value and differentiation reside. The second tool, the core capability grid, can help you separate those activities that are clearly core (create value, drive differentiation, important in the profit pools, strategic to own) from those that are not. The third framework, the gap analysis, can help you clarify the state of the most important capabilities. It helps you answer two questions: what is your capability gap compared with your key competitors (positive or negative)? What is the

Defining Your Core Capabilities

Once you have defined your value chain, you can ask the following seven questions to identify and characterize your core capabilities:

1. Which steps drive the most value from the point of view of our customer?

2. Which steps are associated with the largest profit pools?

3. What are the capabilities in the most important parts of the value chain?

4. In which capabilities are we significantly differentiated compared with our competitors? Why is that?

5. How much of our profit is attributable to those differentiations?

6. Can we measure this advantage and its trajectory (growing or declining)?

7. How might this picture change in the future?

---

trajectory (widening or narrowing) over time? The final chart, the capability investment plan, can help you identify those capabilities that you need to acquire or need to strengthen through investment.

Together, the four charts can provide a valuable picture of your capabilities. The process of assembling the pieces is certain to generate ideas, suggest new strategic options, or shed light on the requirements for some of the known options.

One European company had a portfolio of strong business positions in low-growth and consolidating markets that were encountering impending limits to growth. Yet the company was generating an abundance of cash and in the past had always been able to earn attractive returns by entering new, related businesses or spawning subcores in niche markets. These still existed, but there seemed to be fewer of them on the horizon than before.

The company undertook a three-pronged effort. The first project identified all the known possibilities for creating one or more new cores. The second used a process like the one described here to identify the most important and differentiated capabilities in the company and to examine where they might be reapplied, extending and projecting these leadership strengths into new areas. These lists were brought together and filtered through a series of screens (size of the profit pool, extent of differentiation, relatedness to the existing cores, difficulty of implementation, and potential forms of entry). The management team ended up with three areas of opportunity to pursue. The company is now implementing this strategy, with the eventual goal of redefining its investment profile and renewing core growth.

A quick rundown of some of our case studies shows that strategy redefinition can be triggered by untapped capabilities at virtually any step of the value chain, with the leverage dependent on the customer details and the industry profit pool. For instance, consider a few of the twenty categories:

- *Logistics.* Li & Fung was founded in 1906 as one of the first Chinese-financed trading companies focusing on the export of products like silk, jade, ivory, and fireworks. However, eventually the concept of a trading company reached its limits of sustainability. The company needed to be reinvented— and was, by Victor and William Fung, the grandsons of the founder. They recognized that Li & Fung had a hidden asset in its knowledge of and proprietary access to the broad, complex maze of specialized manufacturing plants throughout China. Over the past twenty-five years, Li & Fung has turned into one of the leading logistics-management companies in the world—a remarkable transformation based on a set of underexploited capabilities. This is a textbook example of a tiny company completely redefining itself based on insights about the company's most differentiated capabilities from the past, combined with an equally powerful intuition about where the future profit pool and customer needs would be shifting.

- *Market Analysis.* The renewal of Procter & Gamble is a text-book case of a large and complex company turning around its performance and refocusing its strategy on the basics, returning underused capabilities for consumer insight to center stage. The new CEO, who had spent most of his career working on core brands such as Tide and finding hidden assets in old brands, recognized the importance of capabilities and was convinced that some existed even at the corporate level.

- *Management Systems.* The repeatable strategy that Danaher used to become the envy of most medium-sized, multicore companies can be traced, in large part, to the embedded capabilities referred to as the Danaher Business System. The company has proven that the system has a reliable impact on the performance of certain types of industrial acquisitions. Before the acquisition strategy was in high gear, the potential for this set of management capabilities was not obvious. It took testing, continual refinement, and redefinition to develop it.

- *Finance.* The remarkable story of GE Capital has multiple origins. The most important one is the development of an internal capability to help customers finance and lease General Electric manufactured products, starting with appliances and then moving into industrial products. This truly hidden capability was picked up by Jack Welch and his team because, though small, it was one of the most profitable parts of the company. They explored how it was possible to do more of it, discovering that they could do it as well as anyone in a highly unconsolidated market.

- *Product Design and Development.* The long and profitable growth trajectory of Novozymes can be told as a story of two kinds of capabilities: those that were untapped (the ability to use knowledge of the first enzyme products to find other commercially viable enzymes) and those that could be added to the mix as science evolved. Being the first to add and commercialize those capabilities is a competitive advantage. The capability of turning a one-product business into a company with a formula to attack a series of niche markets was there all along, but it was unrecognized until it was brought to the fore by the CEO and his team.

- *Services.* In this arena, we turn again to the reinvention of IBM. It sprang from a small services business that took on a life of its own, leading the new CEO to recognize it as a set of capabilities that could move from a support role to center stage. The recognition of its potential emerged from direct discussions between the office of the CEO and zealots in the business unit.

Acquiring Capabilities

Often, the best way to obtain a set of missing capabilities is to acquire them, especially if they are extensive, complex, and difficult to build from scratch and if your industry is evolving rapidly. Biotechnology is an example.

That was the situation for pharmaceutical company Roche, whose risky biotechnology acquisitions have served as the catalysts to transform the company. Roche bought 60 percent of biotech leader Genentech and key assets of Cetus Corporation, owner of critical patents on polymerase chain reaction technology. (Coincidentally, PerkinElmer acquired some elements of this same technology when it bought Applied Biosystems.) At the time of the Genentech purchase, Roche CEO Fritz Gerber said, "It's a lot of money for very little profit, but very little money for such excellent R&D. The returns will be much better than if we had put the money into our own research activities."[7]

After the acquisition, Roche did not interfere with Genentech's strategy, instead seeing its new prize as a capability from which to draw (or add) science and ideas. Roche maintained that approach even as it continued to increase its stake, eventually purchasing the remaining shares. (Roche later offered a portion of the shares to the public, and Genentech is again traded on the New York Stock Exchange.)

Owning Genentech and Cetus's assets heightened Roche's awareness of the growing convergence of diagnostics and pharmaceutical science based on molecular biology. For instance, the company realized that biotech-based drugs for type 2 hepatitis were effective in only 30 to 40 percent of patients. To understand the mechanism for predicting which patients would and would not respond to treatment, doctors needed diagnostic tests at the molecular level of biomarkers, a science closely related to the science in the drug itself. The linkage of diagnostic and therapeutic science is much tighter in the world of biotechnology, where the disease mechanism is the fundamental building block of product design, than in traditional pharmaceuticals.

Understanding this, in 1997 Roche decided to build up its diagnostics business by purchasing Boehringer Mannheim, thereby becoming the world leader in diagnostics systems and products. Though Roche bought Boehringer Mannheim for its marketing muscle, the acquisition also gave Roche a foothold in the fastest-growing and most promising segment of diagnostics: pharmacogenomics, the field of genetic testing and molecular diagnostics. Now Roche is the clear leader in that emerging market—a case, so far, in which the separate acquisitions of capabilities in diagnostics and biotechnology were combined to create a new and highly promising core.

When Roche sold its original over-the-counter drug business (which dated back to 1896) and its market-leading vitamin business, the transformation of the core was complete. Of the top twenty pharmaceutical companies, Roche is in the top three in revenues from biotechnology; some 50 percent of its drug revenues come from biotech. Since 1990, revenues have grown at 9 percent and operating income at 13 percent per year, driving market value up to $110 billion, more than four times the company's revenues at the end of 2004.

The structural changes have allowed Roche to double its profit margins to 23 percent, and analysts expect that profits will only increase as Roche draws on its rich new-product pipeline. Indeed, the before-and-after snapshot of Roche has been called by analysts "the best fundamental story in the sector." It reflects the power of investing preemptively in capabilities, of combining capabilities to create new possibilities in the core, and of shedding businesses and capabilities that no longer fit the new equation. During the full sixteen-year span of this example, Roche has increased its market value thirteen-fold, compared with fourfold for the S&P index of pharmaceutical companies and only threefold for the overall S&P 500 index.

More than 80 percent of the cases of core redefinition in our ten-year *Fortune* 500 study included acquisitions. Depending on definitions, between 5 and 10 percent of those cases involved the addition of major new cores that changed the nature of the company's core, as in the Roche example. Acquisitions also figured significantly in sixteen of the twenty-five detailed case studies used in this book.

However, only two of the twenty-five included acquisitions that created large and distinct new cores in businesses different from the original core and that were intended to form a platform for the next wave of transformation. The second of these, after Roche, was GUS, whose acquisition of the Argos retail chain proved to be key to the development of the new core that led to the transformation of the entire group (see chapter 3). Four other cases included major acquisitions that coexisted with the original core but had a less transforming role: Li & Fung acquiring Inchcape Buying Services (which doubled its size), Nike moving into the broader footwear market by acquiring Cole Haan, Avis vaulting to number 1 on the airport in rental cars by acquiring Budget, and IBM making major acquisitions in services, such as the purchase of PwC Consulting.

The other ten cases involved a series of smaller acquisitions designed to obtain needed capabilities for the transformation, but not the formation of an immediate, distinct new core. Adding capabilities through acquisition in this way has the effect of bringing formerly distant, adjacent market opportunities within reach, and a string of such moves can redefine the strategy of a business.

Pitfalls in Redefining Through Capabilities

Less than 20 percent of the examples of redefinition that we studied used one, or a few, underleveraged capabilities (possibly in combination with a few new ones) as the primary driver of the new strategy. More than 80 percent derived their primary thrust from an underexploited platform (chapter 3) or from redesigning some of the fundamentals of their model to serve core customers (chapter 4). Yet in almost all of these cases, capabilities are found in important supporting roles even if they are seldom found in the lead.

Redefining through underexploited capabilities, or through untapped combinations of old and new capabilities, presents difficulties and traps that are important to understand. We noted five such traps:

- *Overestimating the strength of your capability.* Reasons: wrong benchmarks, corporate narcissism.

- *Underestimating the challenge of building a new capability.* Reasons: insufficient sense of what it is to be world class, an insufficiently aggressive investment plan. Perhaps the remarkable strategic failure of Sony versus Samsung and Apple in some areas of consumer products can be explained by insufficient software capabilities developed by Sony, perhaps misjudging the massive effort that was needed to retool.

- *Building a capability of insufficient quality or capacity for the future.* Reasons: failure to think dynamically about the levels that will be needed in the future, insufficient attention to capability investments being made by competitors. Part of the story of Wal-Mart's triumph over Kmart can be told in terms of systems and information capabilities of the former versus the distraction and underinvestment of the latter.

- *Misunderstanding the linkage to the core and becoming distracted.* Reasons: underestimating the demands on the capability, assuming people can do multiple jobs at once, splitting assignments for convenience but failing to realize the ineffectiveness of this tactic.

- *Imprecise definition of capabilities.* Reason: insufficient research into the details of what is really needed. Many attempts to move from products to services fail because of an insufficiently rich understanding of the various types of service capabilities.

In all these cases, the recognition of hidden capabilities and their locations within the business came from a deliberate search for ways to create a new wave of growth and from a mind-set for change. Finding them required specific data on the strength and effectiveness of the targeted capability. In my experience, a calculated process to find out what your capabilities are, to diagnose their effectiveness, and to remain vigilant about any changes will increase your sightings of hidden assets and their corollary hidden opportunities.

When all else fails, retreat to simplicity and see whether you have agreement to this question: "What are we the best at doing, and why?" Then see where that leads.

Identifying How Core Capabilities Have Untapped Potential

How do you go from identifying and evaluating your core capabilities to determining which of them might play a key role in the next generation strategy?

Formulating strategy for the future requires finding situations where three things are true simultaneously: (1) your strategy focuses on the pursuit of a strong and sustainable profit pool; (2) your strategy holds the potential to be highly differentiated relative to your competition in a way that's hard to match; and (3) you can execute on the plan rapidly and with high probability of success.

Recent research that we have conducted across a large sample of strategy studies for clients at Bain & Company indicates that those are the three non-negotiable requirements to achieve profitability from a strategy. A core capability can have untapped potential to be a linchpin for a new strategy in five ways:

- *Doubling Down:* Where a major investment in a core capability, raising it to a new level, can turn it into a decisive source of competitive advantage in the new strategy. (Example: How IBM invested in its service business.)

- *Extension:* Where a core capability can be extended to a completely different (new) market or use. (Example: How Apple used its design, software, and customer capabilities to create the iPod and its strategy.)

- *Projection:* Where a core capability can be combined with assets from outside your company (possibly by an acquisition) to create something new and unique. (Example: How Roche was able to leverage its purchase of Genentech to improve its traditional pharmaceutical business, to establish a division in pharmacogenomics, and to shift the center of gravity of its value creation towards biotechnology-related products.)

- *Combination:* Where one of your core capabilities can combine with capabilities that you already possess elsewhere in the company to create something wholly new. (Example: How Boston Scientific combined new and old elements in its stent strategy.)

- *Elevation:* Where a once-strong capability has been subordinated or diluted, and that could, if revived and highlighted, drive a new strategy. (Example: Applera's knowledge and patents to serve the market for genetic sequencing was a hidden asset of core capabilities.)

Seldom does the right answer emerge just from having a few people discuss it in a conference room. What's usually needed is a wide range of new perspectives and direct contact with the marketplace. Finding underutilized capabilities and establishing how to use them requires involvement from many levels of the organization, some fresh data (such as the relative strength of core capabilities), and a creative process for developing the strategic choices and refining them depending on discoveries that are made regarding hidden assets.

6

_____

Managing Through
the Growth Cycle

Redefinition is hard, and sometimes it is surprising. Who would have believed that Michael Jordan, perhaps the best athlete on the planet for a while, would have floundered as he did when he tried to redefine his sports career by moving from basketball to baseball? After Jordan signaled an end to his ill-fated baseball career, _Sports Illustrated_ crowed:

> Granted, he looks good in a baseball uniform. Granted, he is the greatest basketball player who has ever lived. . . . But this much is clear: Michael Jordan has no more business patrolling right field in Comiskey Park than Minnie Minoso has bringing the ball upcourt for the Chicago Bulls. The single most impressive thing Jordan has done on a baseball field occurred shortly before his first official spring training game, last Friday in Sarasota, Fla. He and some of the other White Sox were taking BP on an out-of-the-way diamond—Minnie Minoso Field, to be exact—when it came time to collect the baseballs and put them in a basket on the mound. Much to the delight of a small crowd, Jordan started shooting fallaway

jumpers with the balls. For the sake of posterity and those basketball fans who miss him, it should be noted that Jordan was 5 for 7 from the field.[1]

Shortly after this, Jordan left baseball and returned to the basketball court—a game that, arguably, he had a hand in redefining. If this kind of redefinition—an athlete with almost superhuman skills trying a new sport—is difficult, imagine the challenge of redefining a non-superhuman organization with thousands of employees and hundreds of processes directed at fulfilling a strategy that needs to be changed significantly.

In the introduction to this book, I mentioned a Chinese proverb: "Sometimes to be reborn, you first must die." This saying is disproved by many of the cases we looked at. These businesses survived and were reborn, transforming from unsustainable to unstoppable, at least for a time. Yet the level of success in these examples is not the rule but the exception. For all companies that try to redefine, we estimate that the success rate is probably about one in five. And the trends—bankruptcies, CEO departures, the average life span of companies—suggest that it is becoming more difficult.

When it happens, the value of adapting an existing organization to profound change—rather than letting it languish and decay—can be great. I estimate that at the time our twenty-five examples recognized the need to make fundamental changes in the cores, their combined market value was about $50 billion; after the change was executed, it rose in value by a factor of ten, to about $500 billion. Obviously, the company that develops the skills to manage through the focus-expand-redefine cycle repeatedly in all its product lines will do much better than the company that does not learn how to adapt. But it is never instantaneous nor free of cost. The typical time to recognize, execute, and reap the results of a new strategy was three to four years, although it can vary by industry and company circumstance.

Major change often requires strong motivation. Twelve of the renewal programs were formulated by new CEOs brought in to rejuvenate the strategy. Ten of the twenty-five companies (Harman

International, Marvel Entertainment, Li & Fung, Samsung, TACA, Hyperion, Avis, American Express, IBM, and Brunswick) were in or just entering a crisis in the core when they began to make broad changes. Another eight were heading toward potential stall-out. The other seven saw more distant signs for concern. Turbulence was the rule and not the exception; few mustered the impetus to change without a burning platform and a mandate.

Four Lessons in Redefining with Hidden Assets

The image etched by our data is somewhat somber—but with bright bands of hope amid dark passages that beckon the unwary. This mixed picture is not surprising. Only one in ten companies achieves even a modest level of sustained and profitable growth over a decade, and that percentage is declining over time as the growth cycle speeds up. When businesses stall out, fewer than one in five manages to revive its growth rates, and the odds of stalling out increase with size, age, and complexity. Finally, only about 20 to 25 percent of companies in turbulent industries that face the imperative to redefine their core strategy are able to earn for their employees and shareholders another successful ride on the carousel of growth, the focus-expand-redefine cycle. What's a company to do?

As we have seen, sometimes tragically, the answer is seldom delivered by the intoxicating, or numbing, magic elixirs of business—big-bang transforming moves, leaps into sexy new markets, pursuit of the next big idea, or retreats to the familiar comfort of the status quo with the hope that it will all go away in the morning. When you stand back from it all, four main themes of strategy emerge from our seven-year study of the growth, renewal, and decline of companies. These strategies were central to most cases of renewal.

The first theme is the primacy of achieving a deep understanding of the core of your business (see the state of the core diagnostic discussed in chapter 2) combined with a reluctance to leap far into the unknown unless absolutely necessary—a conviction that somehow the core or its new and improved version remains key to the future. The second theme is a willingness to shed dead-end businesses or products, even to shrink to grow, so you can focus on and nurture more promising cores. That approach was effective in kick-starting the process of change in companies like Samsung, PerkinElmer, GUS, and even IBM (which recently sold its PC business).

The third main theme is a passion for operational excellence and low-cost economics as a platform for growth. Virtually no cases of long-term value creation or repeated renewal were built on decaying or inefficient operating platforms. Operational excellence alone is not a substitute for strategy, because strategy provides a road map to the future, a clear customer focus, a determination of how you are differentiated compared with your competitors. But operational excellence is an essential ingredient in nearly all the lasting, great strategies or strategic rejuvenations in the history of business.

The final theme is to build the renewal from components you already possess or can readily obtain. This is the path of hidden assets. Most of this book has focused one-by-one on each of the three categories of hidden assets—customer, platform, and capabilities—but certain critical success factors apply universally and provide a fitting way to end this final summary of the lessons from *Unstoppable.*

Lesson 1: Redefinition Starts with the Core Customer

Virtually all the successful examples were built on a clear concept of the core customer at the center of the new strategy. The focus might be on reinventing the service model to existing customers or on shifting the definition of the core customer. But it was never about a hot market, an abstract technology, or a big strategic idea that came out of the blue. The redefinitions that worked were grounded in the detailed behavioral patterns and economics of specific, identifiable core customers. This principle held whether the key hidden asset was a customer asset, a new platform, a capability, or a combination of the three.

Lesson 2: To Drive Redefinition, Hidden Assets Must Satisfy Four Conditions

Successful strategic renewals using hidden assets satisfied four criteria: (1) clear and measurable competitive differentiation, (2) tangible value added for the customer, (3) a robust (and often new) profit pool, and (4) the ability to obtain the needed capabilities for implementation. Like the four essentials of a good golf swing, each of the four essentials of strategic renewal sounds doable on its own and not very daunting. The difficulty comes in doing all of them at one time and then repeating it over and over.

Lesson 3: Seeing Hidden Assets Requires New Lines of Sight

Hidden assets were seldom physically out of sight. Rather it was their potential that was not recognized, nor how that potential might be released. We observed two primary challenges to recognizing such "hidden obviousness." One is the difficulty of cracking through the mental screens and biases that underpin our view of the world and our own situation. The psychological literature of group decision making—such as the classic *Groupthink* by Irving Janis—characterizes well the pernicious effect of collective bias and selective blindness to the truth. These behaviors are especially pervasive, and costly, under stress and rapidly changing outside conditions. The biases are magnified in groups that have been successful in the past, a pattern we saw in some of the stories of disappointment or disaster. Successful redefinition, I now believe, starts with having the right mind-set to see what is possible and to question the successful patterns of the past.

The other challenge is to find the right new vantage points from which to obtain a fresh perspective on your business and its assets. This point of view might come from customers, new employees, or people on the outside. Notably, some of the best insights about hidden assets were by new CEOs during their first one hundred days on the job, from people who are close observers of other industries and their patterns, or from frontline employees who see the customer every day (but seldom are consulted for strategic insights). We saw this in PerkinElmer (new CEO), Marvel and De Beers (observing other business patterns), and Apple (fresh product perspectives that broke the mold).

Lesson 4: Using Hidden Assets May Require Redefining the Organization

This book is first about strategy, and not organization, not management technique, not implementation planning. Yet these dimensions often are as important as the strategy itself. In the case of renewed strategies for a core business using hidden assets—elements resident elsewhere in the organization but undervalued or used for other purposes—the organizational issues can be unusual and require the investment of senior management time.

Five questions bear asking that line up against some of the key enablers and inhibitors that we observed throughout the case studies.

- Should we set up a focused and dedicated program office to monitor and drive the change process?

- How can I ensure that learning and course correction happen as we embark into new territory?

- Is the turbulence in our industry symptomatic of a general acceleration? How can I increase the speed and metabolism of my decision processes under the new strategy?

- What new or improved capabilities are needed for implementation? What is the plan to obtain them?

- What key decisions need to be made about the new strategy and the assets that enable it? Should those decisions be made differently than before? How?

Profiting from the Core

This chapter concludes my series of three books exploring how companies find new sources of profitable growth. The first, *Profit from the Core*, examines the topic of strategic focus and describes how businesses that seem to have all the ingredients for profitable growth somehow lose their way. The second, *Beyond the Core*, looks at the various ways that businesses find growth opportunities surrounding their core business, pushing out the boundaries step by step into adjacent areas. A long period of adjacency expansion may result in true transformation of the business. It's like the gradual growth from childhood to adulthood, something that always leaves parents wondering when it all happened.

Unstoppable completes the cycle (which my two sons call "the core trilogy"). Here, the focus has been on how businesses make fundamental changes in their cores—by adding new capabilities that push out the boundaries, by shifting the center of gravity of the core to a new location, or by switching the core entirely.

The evidence suggests that management teams will increasingly confront the question of what to do when the core is not enough. Industries are more turbulent. Cycle times of strategies are universally declared to be speeding up. The shelf life of competitive and customer data is decreasing. Capital and information are shifting faster than ever. Leaders hold market positions more tenuously. CEOs are churning through their jobs at a record pace. Most important, sources of competitive differentiation are, on average, more fleeting than they once were.

For many companies, formerly responsive planning systems are no longer sufficiently rapid, adaptable, and insightful. This is a contributing factor to the many cases cited throughout the three books of companies that reacted too late, failed to react, or lurched in desperation toward a big-bang solution that turned out to be another big bust.

I am often asked about the best practice for managing strategic planning and resource allocation. This is the process of monitoring the environment, tracking the key indicators for each business, and surfacing the right strategic options when change (at any stage of the focus-expand-redefine cycle) is called for. The answer, I believe, is that there are many varieties of "systems," just as there are many varieties of playing styles of Hall of Fame tennis players, of the world-class conductors of symphony orchestras, or of great architects. However, each discipline seems to have its own core principles that define success. The same is true of business.

Based on seven years of research and analysis of case studies and discussion of these findings in many management meetings, I believe that the best systems should take into account, in their own way, the following ten principles, findings, and observations.

Ten Principles of Core Growth and Redefinition

1. Start by Defining the Core

2. Obsess on the Full Potential of the Core

3. Fully Value Leadership Economics

4. Map Out Adjacencies to the Core

5. Recognize the Power of Repeatability in the Core

6. When Lost, Return to the Core Customer

7. Remember the Focus-Expand-Redefine Cycle of Growth

8. Exploit the Power of Hidden Assets

9. Think of Capabilities as the Building Blocks of Renewal

10. Don't Underestimate the Power of Focus

1. Start by Defining the Core
(*Profit from the Core,* Chapters 1 and 2)

If you do not understand your core (or cores), the root cause of your strategic differentiation, how you really earn economic profit (and why), and the boundaries of your core, then trying to do anything else is a waste of time. At off-site meetings with executives, I'm constantly surprised by how many relatively sophisticated companies seem to have lost a sense of their core—and how many have never even talked about it. If you're not sure who you are, it's hard to decide what you want to become and what it is worth.

Ask yourself how long it has been since you talked at length about the boundaries of the core or the root cause of differentiation several levels down—or, better yet, since you made a full assessment of the state of the core itself. What did your assessment say?

2. Obsess on the Full Potential of the Core
(*Profit from the Core,* Chapter 2)

One of the greatest mistakes in business is to prematurely abandon the core in search of hot new markets, technologies, or opportunities. Our surveys show repeatedly that more than 60 percent of executives say that their core business is not within 50 percent of its full potential for profitable growth. Yet most of them are not sure where that potential lies.

What is the full potential of your core? How do you know? These two questions need to be at the top of the agenda of any system for evaluating growth opportunities in companies.

3. Fully Value Leadership Economics (*Profit from the Core,* Chapter 2; *Beyond the Core,* Chapter 6)

Everyone knows that it is far more valuable to be the leader in a market and to control the profit pool. Positions of leadership, even in subsegments of your business, may be more valuable than you realize. Usually a core of leadership economics accounts for most of the value of a company.

Accounting systems act to obscure the power of leadership economics, and many of the attributes that are cataloged in chapter 2 in *Profit from the Core* are not fully appreciated. This is true not only in finding the launching pad for transformation but also in appraising the odds of success of an adjacent move, or even in assessing the value of investing in pure market share.

Ask yourself whether you are absolutely sure that you understand the true boundaries and profit economics of your leadership positions.

4. Map Out Adjacencies to the Core
   (*Beyond the Core,* Chapter 1)

The average strong core business might have as many as seventy to one hundred investment opportunities that radiate around it. It makes no sense at all to pursue most of them. The question, then, is which to pursue and when.

Often, these adjacency opportunities hold the clues to broader strategic themes that might suggest adding a capability into the core. Often, they have their roots in customer requests, in ways that leading customers are using the product, in next-generation needs, or in ideas from suppliers—the front lines of future market requirements. For the typical adjacent move the odds of success are only 25 percent. Thus, it is crucial to establish clear, agreed-upon criteria and make adjacency evaluation and data collection part of the process. The science of management has refined cost reduction and quality improvement to a high level. The management approaches to growth investments are much more primitive, and yet they are at least as important, maybe more so.

Ask yourself whether you know the criteria for investing in adjacencies and how to compare alternative growth investments.

5. Recognize the Power of Repeatability in the Core
(*Beyond the Core,* Chapter 3)

One of the most consistent characteristics of the best sustained-growth companies is that they have developed a repeatable growth formula that fuels their adjacent moves or that even characterizes their additions of new capabilities to evolve the core over time. Nike epitomizes this through its movement from one sport to another and, within sports, with its product choreography from shoes to products centered on sports icons to soft goods, sometimes to hard goods, and then to specialty channels. Vodafone's geographic expansion was strengthened by its repeatability. GE Capital's 170 acquisitions in the leasing business are the essence of acquisition-based repeatability. Dell's ability to establish the direct model across segments, products, and geographies was the engine of its growth. Some companies, such as Li & Fung and Novozymes, repeatedly added capabilities that let them redefine their scope and ultimately redefine their core.

Ask yourself whether you value this attribute highly enough, and discuss it in management meetings and strategy sessions.

6. When Lost, Return to the Core Customer
(*Beyond the Core,* Chapters 2 and 3)

We found that more than 80 percent of the best adjacency ideas in successful companies came from (or related to) the core customer and not from the lab or the corporate office, the world of investment bankers, or even creative off-site sessions. There are five main lenses for X-raying customers. Some companies use them well and productively, and others just go through the motions. These lenses are the customer life cycle of purchases, customer system economics, customer segmentation, customer share of wallet and purchasing patterns, and your own customer adjacencies.

The odds of success for customer-led adjacencies are higher than for others. When in doubt about what to do, return to first principles and drill down to the core customer. The best ideas come from drilling down into the core like an anthropologist studying behavior, and not from scanning the outside for big ideas. With shrinking competitor differentiations, the ability to find microsegment opportunities and gain insight faster than competitors provides enormous advantage.

Ask yourself whether you think you are world class in obtaining new customer insights compared with your competitors.

7. Remember the Focus-Expand-Redefine Cycle of Growth (*Unstoppable,* Chapters 1 and 2)

Some of the most profound strategic miscalculations relate to decisions about whether to focus on the full potential of your core, whether to invest heavily in adjacencies, and whether to redefine the core (or even move to or add another core). Premature abandonment of the core, as in the case of Bausch & Lomb years ago, can be as devastating as sticking with an eroding core for too long, as Polaroid did. Both of these companies were once darlings of Wall Street, both had intelligent management teams, and both had a formerly dominant core. And both made miscalculations at either end of the focus-expand-redefine cycle.

In your planning for the next wave of growth, do you probe in a balanced way into each phase? Are you still sure where you are? What are the warning signals you look for?

8. Exploit the Power of Hidden Assets (*Unstoppable,* Chapters 3–5)

Two-thirds of companies will encounter a crisis in the core in the next decade, a crisis that will raise fundamental questions about the need to redefine their strategies. Moreover, those who wait too long and stall out for an extended period will trigger a series of downward-pointing dynamics that will further inhibit the desired rebound.

Basic strategic change is hard to decide on and even harder to implement. Risks are high even for the earliest and the best. So it is important to learn lessons from other experiences and even other industries. One lesson is that nearly all the cases of business renewal that we examined were built using hidden assets that were not central to the past but became more critical than before. One example is underused customer data, such as the data that helped rejuvenate American Express and set it on a fifteen-year growth run. Another example is a support activity to the core that has the potential to become a separate and important core business in its own right. The turnaround of IBM via IBM Global Services is such an example.

Managing the strategic balance sheet—including hidden assets, hidden liabilities, and strategic equity—is the first job of a CEO and management team; they need to recognize that many of the most important liabilities in the present, and assets for the future, are often hidden from view and need to be pursued and uncovered.

9. Think of Capabilities as the Building Blocks of Renewal (*Unstoppable,* Chapter 5)

Adding the right new capability, with sufficient force and power, can magnify the power of the core, rejuvenate a flagging growth model, and push out the boundaries of the core into new, previously unreachable areas. We saw this throughout the examples in this book. In some businesses it is almost as if the organization, and its ability to add capabilities, is the strategy itself. Organization is the new strategy. How about that?

Are you spending enough time taking inventory of existing capabilities, which are the most critical to differentiation, and assessing how they currently stack up and which need to be added?

10. Don't Underestimate the Power of Focus (All Three Books, All Chapters)

In its own way, each of my three books has as its dominant theme the power of focus. Focus to grow sounds almost counterintuitive. But just as plants often must be cut back to concentrate their energy on fewer, stronger branches, so too, businesses must be pruned to counter their tendency to branch out more than they should. I'm constantly amazed by how often the correct first step to growth and expansion is to narrow the focus.

Profit from the Core is about the strategic focus of a core business. It is based on hundreds of examples we found of businesses that lost their opportunities by becoming unfocused and losing track of what the few things at the center of their core really were. *Beyond the Core* is also about focus, but in a different way. It shows that following a repeatable formula is the best way to reduce risk as well as a powerful organizing principle behind profitable growth. The pursuit of repeatability based on a strong core is a formula for focusing and concentrating resources.

Unstoppable is about transformation and renewal, but it conveys a central message that is about focus in yet another sense: focus to understand and build on the hidden assets you already have. If you can do that, you have a better chance of success and differentiation than if you leap into something completely new. Furthermore, for companies struggling to reignite growth, one of the most under-used and most reliable ways to create economic value is to consider narrowing focus and even shrinking in order to grow.

The world serves up a never-ending series of temptations, distractions, doubts, and uncertainties. It is possible for management teams to bounce like ping-pong balls from one topic or issue to another, never digging in and understanding their core and what it means. The real focus of businesses should be external—on competitors, shifts in technology, and customer dynamics. Yet my overwhelming feeling from seven years of studying success and failure among companies searching for profitable growth is that, ironically, many of the most challenging demons are internal and our most difficult foes are often ourselves. The following are also true:

> If you do not know yourself, it is difficult to judge what you should become.

> If you do not know where you are, it is difficult to decide where to go and how.

If you do not know what you are really good at, it is tough to know what to do.

The starting place in each of the three phases of the focus-expand-redefine cycle of business growth is to make sure that you understand and are profiting from your core.

Do you? Are you?

APPENDIX

Methodology

This book is based on data from a series of related analyses and surveys. The purpose of these analyses was to understand four aspects of business redefinitions:

- The frequency of various paths to redefinition

- The odds of success and failure of various pathways and choices

- The barriers to decision and implementation

- The pace of change

The key sources of data and analysis, and the essence of the methods, are as follows.

1. Fortune 500 Analysis

Purpose: To assess the degree of change across companies (especially single-core companies) over time and to estimate the relative frequency of various patterns.

Method: We tracked the five hundred largest U.S. public companies from 1995 through 2004. We determined how many of this group had gone bankrupt and how many had been acquired by other companies and absorbed. Acquisition is not necessarily a negative event, but it is a significant structural change for the acquired company. We then took a 50 percent sample of the remaining two hundred eighty companies and did a more extensive ten-year before-and-after profile. Our judgment about the extent of change hinged on the answers to three questions:

- Was there a significant change in financial performance?

- Was there significant structural change in the company, its core, and its sources of advantage?

- Was there significant change in how close observers described the company and its strategy?

2. Analysis of Redefinition Patterns

Purpose: To empirically examine broad patterns of company change.

Method: From the sample of one hundred forty companies, we separated out conglomerates (there were 25) so that we could focus on single-core companies or companies with a set of related and interlinked cores in the same general industry. We wanted to look at the phenomenon of business-level changes as distinct from portfolio churn across many unrelated businesses.

Our team then examined before-and-after changes in a series of lengthy discussion sessions. We began with a large number of fine gradations, defined by looking at the data case by case. As we proceeded, however, we realized that the distinctions were blurring and collapsing into each other. For instance, a company that redefined itself by making a significant move from products to services (one category of redefinition) also often changed its organization to focus more on "solutions" or "systems" than on single components. There were many such cases. As a result, we collapsed our categories of change to those that we felt were most meaningful:

- Redefinition through a series of directional adjacent moves that stretched and changed the core over time

- Redefinition through one or more fundamental changes in the business model, usually the model of serving the core customer

- Creation of new cores or adoption of a formula to spawn multiple new cores

3. Analysis of Big-Bang Redefinitions

Purpose: To examine the nature and success rate of large-scale, dramatic transforming moves.

Method: We did an extensive literature search of the business press from 1995 to 2002, searching for words that signified transformation or redefinition. We supplemented this search with analysis of the Bain database of case studies.

Eventually we chose fifteen cases to study, each one large in magnitude and sudden in implementation. Usually these were mergers, such as AOL/Time Warner, or a series of large acquisitions along a theme, such as Monsanto's attempt to shuck its core in chemicals and become a biotechnology company.

The list of companies we selected to study is as follows:

AT&T (convergence strategy leading to cable and wireless acquisitions)

Compaq (services strategy, acquisition of Digital Equipment Corporation services)

ConAgra (movement into branded products)

Daimler-Benz (Chrysler and product transformation)

Deutsche Post (movement into logistics and express services)

Hewlett-Packard (Compaq merger)

ICI (movement from commodity to specialty chemicals)

Loral (telecom)

LVMH (movement into general retail)

Mattel (Learning Company strategy)

McKesson (acquisition of HBOC and movement into IT)

Merck (Medco and distribution strategy)

Monsanto (biotech acquisition strategy)

Time Warner (AOL merger)

Walt Disney (Cap Cities and related media expansions)

For each entity, we did the following:

- Examined key analyst comments before the move and for an extended time afterward

- Analyzed stock price performance versus peers, trajectory, and indexes

- Examined financials

- Reviewed the record in the press

We systematically coded each of these dimensions so that we could judge the company's financial performance, its perceived strategic success, and the primary ingredients of that success or failure.

We found that large moves are inferior by a wide margin to more-measured paths to redefinition, especially those that leverage existing hidden assets and drive them to their full potential. The odds of success from big bangs are less than 10 percent.

4. Surveys of Executives

Purpose: To understand executives' current attitudes and concerns regarding growth; to explore their beliefs about barriers to sustained and profitable growth; and to probe the extent to which executives believe that fundamental changes in their core businesses will be required.

Method: Two surveys by Bain & Company in conjunction with the Economist Intelligence Unit. These are surveys of executives who subscribe to the *Economist* online service. The first survey, the 2004 Growth Survey, took place in October 2004 and drew responses from two hundred fifty-nine executives around the world. The second, the 2005 Capability Survey, took place in November 2005 and drew responses from two hundred forty executives. In both, more than one-fourth of respondents were from each of the major business centers—Asia, North America, and Europe—providing good geographic balance.

5. Analysis of Profit from the Core Database

Purpose: To update our statistics on the difficulty of sustained and profitable growth worldwide and use this data as a backdrop for the challenges faced by companies, challenges that impel major change in their core.

Method: Bain & Company maintains a database of more than eight thousand public companies spanning the G-7 economies. More than two thousand of these companies earn more than $500 million in annual revenues. We did extensive analysis of the linked financial records of the two thousand largest companies and used some of that work for this book. The database links not only published financials but also estimated cost of capital and inflation adjustments for each country.

6. Twenty-Five Case Studies

Purpose: To study the detailed decisions, actions, methods, and lessons learned from a cross section of various types of core redefinitions. Many of these are still in process. We attempted to balance contemporary experience with enough history to make early determinations regarding outcome.

Method: We developed an extensive list of companies that had undergone significant core change along three dimensions: financial performance, source of differentiation, and external description of company and strategy. We compiled much of the list by polling all Bain partners who headed industry practice areas and asking about cases of redefinition in their industries. We also mined the Bain database and polled Bain office heads about interesting companies in their geographies.

Using these methods, we compiled a list of eighty companies and selected twenty-five that balanced industry (from computers to refrigerators), geography (eleven countries represented), and type of change (adjacencies, new customer model, new capability). I also chose to include some that are still in process and others with clear outcomes. In twenty-one of the cases I supplemented research on the company's moves, analyst perceptions, financials, and company histories with in-person interviews or visits to the company. In many cases I was able to conduct several sessions' worth of interviews with the senior executives directly involved. For TACA, for instance, I visited El Salvador and interviewed the top four executives. For American Express, I conducted two interviews with CEO Ken Chenault. In a few cases I did not pursue interviews, because the companies' strategy is still in process and extensive written material was available. The full list follows; asterisks indicate in-person visits and interviews.

American Express*	Li & Fung*
Apple*	Marvel Entertainment
Autodesk*	Nike*
Avis*	Novozymes*
Boston Scientific	PerkinElmer/Applera*
Brunswick*	PSA Corporation*
De Beers*	Procter & Gamble*
Dell*	Roche
Dometic*	Royal Vopak*
GUS*	Samsung*
Harman International*	TACA*
Hyperion Solutions*	Tesco*
IBM	

Notes

Chapter 1

1. "DeBeers History, 1900–1940," www.debeersgroup.com.

2. "Diamonds: Crystal Clear?" *Economist*, July 15, 2000.

3. Gareth Penny, interview with author, London, October 18, 2005.

4. "The Big Leap," *Economist*, January 15, 2000.

5. Distance from the core drives the odds of success of movements into adjacencies that companies pursue in search of new growth. One way to measure the distance is in terms of the number of steps (or partial steps) away from the core on five dimensions: same or new customers (one step if completely new customers); same or new channel of distribution; amount of shared infrastructure; use of the key core asset (brand or technology); and shared competitors. When a move is more than about one and a half steps away, the odds of success start to drop at an accelerating rate, signaling greater levels of complexity and unfamiliarity.

Chapter 2

1. Geoffrey Colvin, "Managing in Chaos," *Fortune*, October 2, 2006, 76–82.

2. William T. O'Hara, *Centuries of Success: Lessons from the World's Most Enduring Family Businesses* (Avon, MA: Adams Media, 2004).

3. Orit Gadiesh and James L. Gilbert, "Profit Pools: A Fresh Look at Strategy," and "How to Map Your Industry's Profit Pool," *Harvard Business Review*, May–June 1998, 139–147 and 149–162.

4. Gary Hamel and C. K. Prahalad, *Competing for the Future* (Boston: Harvard Business School Press, 1994), 4.

5. Bob Salerno, interview with author, Parsippany, New Jersey, June 16, 2005.

6. Salerno interview.

7. Salerno interview.

8. NET PROMOTER is a registered trademark of Satmetrix Systems, Inc., Bain & Company, and Fred Reichheld.

9. John Paul Broeders, interview with author, Rotterdam, The Netherlands, June 27, 2006.

10. Chairman Lee, "Dialogue with Employees," March 22, 1998.

Chapter 3

1. Thomas P. Fahy, *Richard Scott Perkin and the Perkin-Elmer Corporation* (Norwalk, CT: Perkin-Elmer Print Shop, 1987).

2. Tony White, interview with author, Atlanta, February 22, 2005.

3. Matt Ridley, *Genome: The Autobiography of a Species in 23 Chapters* (New York, HarperCollins Publishers, 2000).

4. White interview, 2005.

5. Sven Stork, interview with author, Solna, Sweden, September 20, 2005.

6. Louis V. Gerstner, Jr., *Who Says Elephants Can't Dance: Inside IBM's Historic Turnaround* (New York: HarperBusiness, 2002), 129.

7. Isaac Wolfson, *Great Universal Stores: 25 Years of Progress, 1932–1957* (London: Universal House, 1957).

8. John Peace, interview with author, London, June 29, 2005.

9. Noreen O'Leary, "Return of the Shadow," *Chief Executive*, May 1, 1999, 26.

10. Henry Chesbrough, *Open Innovation* (Boston: Harvard Business School Press, 2003).

Chapter 4

1. Dr. Sidney Harman, interview by with author, Washington, D.C., January 31, 2005.

2. Daniel Boorstin, *The Discoverers* (New York: Vintage Press, 1983), 329.

3. "The Autodesk File: Bits of History, Words of Experience," www.fourmilab.ch.

4. John Walker, InfoCorp Silverado Speech, March 2, 1986, www.fourmilab.ch/autofile.

5. Gene G. Marcial, "Inside Wall Street: A High-Tech Issue That May Not Fly," *BusinessWeek,* July 8, 1985, 85.

6. David Lieberman, "Hot Growth Companies: There Are 100 Winners—And As Many Reasons for Their Success," *BusinessWeek,* May 25, 1987, 82.

7. Carl Bass, interview with author, San Rafael, CA, May 20, 2006.

8. Fred Reichheld, *The Ultimate Question: Driving Good Profits and True Growth* (Boston: Harvard Business School Publishing, 2006).

9. Jeffrey Rodek, interview by with author, Santa Clara, CA, May 3, 2006.

10. Ken Chenault, interview by with author, New York, May 24, 2005.

11. Darrell Rigby and Chris Zook, "Open-Market Innovation," *Harvard Business Review*, (October 2002), 80–89.

12. Constantinos C. Markides and Paul A. Geroski, *Fast Second: How Smart Companies Bypass Radical Innovation to Enter and Dominate New Markets* (San Francisco: Jossey-Bass, 2004).

13. Ted Pincus, "Buckley Transforming Brunswick a Third Time," *Chicago Sun-Times*, July 29, 2003, 50.

14. George Buckley, interview by with author, Chicago, January 23, 2005.

Chapter 5

1. Ian MacLaurin, interview by with author, London, January 23, 2005.

2. Gary Hamel and C. K. Prahalad, *Competing for the Future* (Boston: Harvard Business School Press, 1994), 203–204. George Stalk has embellished the idea by distinguishing between a core competence, which tends to emphasize "technological or production expertise at specific points along the value chain," and core capabilities, which are "more broadly based, encompassing the entire value chain. In this respect, capabilities are visible to the customer in a way core competencies rarely are." Stalk and his colleagues Philip Evans and Lawrence E. Shulman went on to describe, in their 1992 article "Competing on Capabilities: The New Rules of Corporate Strategy" (*Harvard Business Review*, March–April 1992, 57–69), how "capabilities-based competition" would characterize the next wave of corporate strategy. It has taken a while for that shift to occur, but as the examples show, it is happening.

3. Michael Porter, "What Is Strategy?" *Harvard Business Review*, November–December 1996, 61–78.

4. Steen Riisgaard, interview by with author, Copenhagen, Denmark, February 14, 2005.

5. Mike Kehoe, interview by with author, Cincinnati, June 20, 2005.

6. J.P. Morgan, Apple Computer, Inc, iPod Economics, November 16, 2004, 6–7.

7. Peter Fuhrman, "No Need for Valium," *Forbes*, January 31, 1994, 84.

Chapter 6

1. Steve Wulf, "Err Jordan," *Sports Illustrated*, March 14, 1994, 20.

Bibliography

Books

Baghai, Mehrdad, Stephen Coley, and David White. *The Alchemy of Growth*. London: Orion Business, 1999.

Bazerman, Max H. *Judgment in Managerial Decision Making*. Hoboken, N.J.: John Wiley & Sons, 2006.

Boorstin, Daniel. *The Discoverers*. New York: Vintage Press, 1983.

Carroll, Glenn R., and Michael T. Hannan. *The Demography of Corporations and Industries*. Princeton, NJ: Princeton University Press, 2000.

Chandler, Alfred D. Jr. *Inventing the Electronic Century: The Epic Story of the Consumer Electronics and Computer Industries*. New York: Free Press, 2001.

Chesbrough, Henry. *Open Innovation*. Boston: Harvard Business School Press, 2003.

Christensen, Clayton M. *The Innovator's Dilemma: When New Technologies Cause Great Firms to Fail*. Boston: Harvard Business School Press, 1997.

Collins, James C., and Jerry I. Porras. *Built to Last: Successful Habits of Visionary Companies*. New York: HarperBusiness, 1997.

Collins, Jim. *Good to Great*. New York: HarperBusiness, 2001.

Csikszentmihalyi, Mihaly. *Flow: The Psychology of Optimal Experience*. New York: Harper Perennial, 1991.

De Bono, Edward. *Lateral Thinking: Creativity Step by Step*. New York: Harper Perennial, 1973.

De Geus, Arie. *The Living Company*. Boston: Harvard Business School Press, 1997.

Dell, Michael, with Catherine Fredman. *Direct from Dell: Strategies That Revolutionized an Industry*. New York: HarperBusiness, 1999.

Fahy, Thomas P. *Richard Scott Perkin and The Perkin-Elmer Corporation*. Norwalk, CT: Perkin-Elmer Print Shop, 1987.

Foster, Richard N. *Innovation: The Attacker's Advantage*. New York: Simon & Schuster, 1988.

Gerstner, Louis V. Jr. *Who Says Elephants Can't Dance: Inside IBM's Historic Turnaround*. New York: HarperBusiness, 2002.

Grove, Andrew S. *Only the Paranoid Survive: How to Exploit the Crisis Points That Challenge Every Company*. New York: Bantam Books, 1999.

Hamel, Gary. *Leading the Revolution*. Boston: Harvard Business School Press, 2000.

Hamel, Gary, and C. K. Prahalad. *Competing for the Future*. Boston: Harvard Business School Press, 1994.

Hannan, Michael T., and John Freeman. *Organizational Ecology*. Boston: Harvard University Press, 1989.

Harding, David, and Sam Rovit. *Mastering the Merger: Four Critical Decisions that Make or Break the Deal*. Boston: Harvard Business School Press, 2004.

Harman, Sidney. *Mind Your Own Business*. New York: Random House, 2003.

Harvard Business Review on Strategies for Growth. Boston: Harvard Business School Press, 1998.

Jacobson, Gary, and John Hillkirk. *Xerox: American Samurai*. New York: MacMillan, 1986.

Janis, Irving L. *Groupthink*. Boston: Houghton Mifflin, 1982.

Kaplan, Robert S., and David P. Norton. *The Balanced Scorecard: Translating Strategy into Action*. Boston: Harvard Business School Press, 1996.

Kim, W. Chan, and Renée Mauborgne. *Blue Ocean Strategy*. Boston: Harvard Business School Publishing, 2005.

Lee, Kun-Hee. *Read the World With Your Own Thinking*. Seoul: The Dong-a-Ilbo, 1997.

Lorsch, Jay W., and Thomas J. Tierney. *Aligning the Stars: How to Succeed When Professionals Drive Results*. Boston: Harvard Business School Press, 2002.

MacLaurin, Ian. *Tiger by the Tail: A Life in Business from Tesco to Test Cricket*. London: Pan Books, 1999.

Markides, Constantinos C., and Paul A. Geroski. *Fast Second: How Smart Companies Bypass Radical Innovation to Enter and Dominate New Markets*. San Francisco: Jossey-Bass, 2004.

Massengill, Reed. *Becoming American Express*. New York: American Express Company, 1999.

O'Hara, William T. *Centuries of Success: Lessons from the World's Most Enduring Family Businesses.* Avon, MA: Adams Media, 2004.

Ormerod, Paul. *Why Most Things Fail: Evolution, Extinction, and Economics.* London: Faber & Faber, 2005.

Plous, Scott. *The Psychology of Judgment and Decision-Making.* New York: McGraw Hill, 1993.

Porter, Michael E. *Competitive Advantage.* New York: Free Press, 1985.

Reichheld, Frederick F. *Loyalty Rules!* Boston: Harvard Business School Press, 2001.

———. *The Loyalty Effect: The Hidden Force Behind Growth, Profits, and Lasting Value.* Boston: Harvard Business School Press, 1996.

———. *The Ultimate Question: Driving Good Profits and True Growth.* Boston: Harvard Business School Press, 2006.

Ridley, Matt. *Genome: The Autobiography of a Species in 23 Chapters.* New York: HarperCollins, 2000.

Rumelt, Richard P., Dan E. Schendel, and David J. Teece, eds. *Fundamental Issues in Strategy: A Research Agenda.* Boston: Harvard Business School Press, 1994.

Schrage, Michael. *Serious Play: How the World's Best Companies Simulate to Innovate.* Boston: Harvard Business School Press, 2000.

Schultz, Howard, and Dori Jones Yang. *Pour Your Heart Into It: How Starbucks Built a Company One Cup at a Time.* New York: Hyperion, 1997.

Shreeve, James. *The Genome War.* New York: Alfred A. Knopf, 2004.

Simon, Hermann. *Hidden Champions: Lessons from 500 of the World's Best Unknown Companies.* Boston: Harvard Business School Press, 1996.

Slater, Robert. *Jack Welch and the GE Way.* New York: McGraw-Hill, 1999.

———. *Saving Big Blue: Leadership Lessons and Turnaround Tactics of IBM's Lou Gerstner.* New York: McGraw Hill, 1999.

Slywotzky, Adrian, and Richard Wise. *How to Grow When Markets Don't.* New York: Warner Business Books, 2003.

Steinbock, Dan. *The Nokia Revolution: The Story of an Extraordinary Company That Transformed an Industry.* New York: AMACOM, 2001.

Stemberg, Thomas G. *Staples for Success.* Santa Monica, CA: Knowledge Exchange, 1996.

Sull, Donald N. *Revival of the Fittest.* Boston: Harvard Business School Press, 2003.

Swasy, Alecia. *Changing Focus: Kodak and the Battle to Save a Great American Company.* New York: Times Business, 1997.

Tellis, Gerard J., and Peter N. Golder. *Will and Vision: How Latecomers Grow to Dominate Markets.* New York: McGraw Hill, 2002.

Utterback, James M. *Mastering the Dynamics of Innovation*. Boston: Harvard Business School Press, 1994.

Wolfson, Isaac. *Great Universal Stores: 25 Years of Progress, 1932–1957*. London: Universal House, 1957.

Zook, Chris. *Beyond the Core*. Boston: Harvard Business School Press, 2004.

Zook, Chris, with James Allen. *Profit from the Core*. Boston: Harvard Business School Press, 2001.

Articles

Abell, Derek F. "Competing Today While Preparing for Tomorrow." *Sloan Management Review* 40, no. 3 (1999): 73–81.

Bank, David, and Gary McWilliams. "Squeeze Play: Picking a Big Fight with Dell, H-P Cuts PC Profits Razor-Thin." *Wall Street Journal*, May 12, 2004.

Baveja, Sarabjit Singh, Jim Gilbert, and Dianne Ledingham. "From Products to Services: Why It's Not So Simple." *Harvard Management Update* 9, no. 4 (2004): 6–8.

Bower, Joseph L., and Clayton M. Christensen. "Disruptive Technologies: Catching the Wave." *Harvard Business Review*, January–February 1995, 43–53.

Chan, Louis K.C., Jason Karceski, and Josef Lakonishok. "The Level and Persistence of Growth Rates." *The Journal of Finance* 58, no. 2 (2003): 643–684.

Chang, Sea-Jin, and Joel Podolny. "Samsung Electronics Semiconductor Division." Case study #IB 24A. Stanford, CA: Stanford Graduate School of Business, 2002.

Charan, Ram, and Geoffrey Colvin. "Why CEOs Fail." *Fortune*, June 21, 1999, 68.

Colvin, Geoffrey, "Managing in Chaos," *Fortune,* October 2, 2006, 76–82.

de Geus, Arie. "The Living Company," *Harvard Business Review*, March–April 1997, 51–54.

"Diamonds: Crystal Clear?" *Economist*, 15 July 2000.

Fuhrman, Peter. "No Need for Valium," *Forbes*, January 31, 1994, 84.

Gadiesh, Orit, and James L. Gilbert. "How to Map Your Industry's Profit Pool." *Harvard Business Review*, May–June 1998, 149–162.

———. "Profit Pools: A Fresh Look at Strategy." *Harvard Business Review*, May–June 1998, 139–147.

Garvin, David A., and Artemis March. "Harvey Golub: Recharging American Express." Case 9-396-212. Boston: Harvard Business School, 1996.

Geroski, Paul A. "Early Warning of New Rivals." *Sloan Management Review* 40, no. 3 (1999): 107–116.

Hamel, Gary and C.K. Prahalad. "The Core Competence of the Corporation." *Harvard Business Review,* May–June 1990, 79–91.

Henry, David. "Mergers: Why Most Big Deals Don't Pay Off." *BusinessWeek*, 14 October 2002, 60–70.

"How to Live Long and Prosper." *Economist*, 10 May 1997.

Kotter, John P. "Leading Change: Why Transformation Efforts Fail." *Harvard Business Review*, March–April 1995, 59–67.

Lajoux, Alexandra Reed, and J. Fred Weston. "Do Deals Deliver on Postmerger Performance?" *Mergers & Acquisitions*, September–October 1998), 34–37.

Lieberman, David. "Hot Growth Companies: There Are 100 Winners—and As Many Reasons for Their Success," *BusinessWeek*, May 15, 1987, 82.

Lucier, Chuck, Rob Schuyt, and Edward Tse. "CEO Succession 2004: The World's Most Prominent Temp Workers." *Strategy+Business*, Summer 2005, http://www.boozallen.de/media/file/ceo_succession_2004.pdf.

"Ma Bell Does the Splits." *Economist*, October 28, 2000.

Marcial, Gene G. "Inside Wall Street: A High-Tech Issue That May Not Fly," *BusinessWeek*, July 6, 1985, 85.

Markides, Constantinos C. "Strategic Innovation." *Sloan Management Review* 38, no. 3, (1997): 9–23.

Markides, Constantinos C. "Strategic Innovation in Established Companies." *Sloan Management Review* 39, no. 1 (1998): 31–42.

Morgan, J.P. Apple Computer, Inc., iPod Economics, November 16, 2004, 6–7.

Morgan, J.P. "GUS: Value in a Wretched Sector." April 8, 2005.

O'Leary, Noreen. "Return of the Shadow." *Chief Executive*, May 1, 1999, 26.

Pincus, Ted. "Buckley Transforming Brunswick a Third Time." *Chicago Sun-Times*, July 29, 2003.

Porter, Michael E. "What Is Strategy?" *Harvard Business Review*, Nov–Dec 1996, 61–78.

Reichheld, Frederick F. "The One Number You Need to Grow." *Harvard Business Review*, December 2003, 46–54.

Rigby, Darrell, and Chris Zook. "Open-Market Innovation." *Harvard Business Review*, October 2002, 80–89.

Roberts, Craig. "Glory Without Growth." *Business Review Weekly*, February 17, 2005.

Stalk, George, Philip Evans, and Lawrence E. Shulman. "Competing on Capabilities: The New Rules of Corporate Strategy." *Harvard Business Review*, March–April 1992, 57–69.

Sull, Donald, Choelsoon Park, and Seonghoon Kim. "Samsung and Daewoo: Two Tales of One City." Case 9-804-055. Boston: Harvard Business School, June 2, 2004.

"The Big Leap." *Economist*, January 15, 2000.

"The Green Gene Giant." *Economist*, April 26, 1997.

Von Braun, Christoph-Friedrich. "The Acceleration Trap." *Sloan Management Review* 32, no. 1 (1990): 49–58.

Wallace, G. David and Scott Scredon, "Hot Growth Companies—The 100 Best with Under $150 Million in Sales," *BusinessWeek*, May 26, 1986, 94–96.

Wulf, Steve. "Err Jordan," *Sports Illustrated*, March 14, 1994, 20.

Index

About the Author

CHRIS ZOOK, a partner at Bain & Company, heads the firm's Global Strategy Practice. During his more than twenty years at Bain, his work has focused on companies searching for new sources of profitable growth, in a wide range of industries.

In 2001 Zook published his best-selling *Profit from the Core* (Harvard Business School Press), which found that nine out of ten companies that had sustained profitable growth for a decade or more had focused on their core businesses, rather than following the siren song of diversification. The book offers an approach to assessing and making the most of core business opportunities. Its sequel, *Beyond the Core* (Harvard Business School Press, 2004), examines how companies that have fully exploited their core businesses can systematically and successfully expand beyond into related, or "adjacent," areas. *Unstoppable* completes the series and examines what to do when a growth formula of the past begins to approach its limits, demanding that the company change its strategic focus and redefine its core.

All three books are based on a growth study begun in 1990 at Bain & Company that involves thousands of companies worldwide. The study's findings have been expanded each year and adopted and applied in hundreds of successful companies in all types of industries.

Zook also writes extensively in the business press, is a frequent speaker at business forums such as the World Economic Forum at Davos, and appears regularly on television and radio. He received a BA from Williams College, an MPhil in Economics from Exeter College, Oxford University, and holds an MPP and a PhD from Harvard University.

He splits his time between homes in Boston and Amsterdam.